GARDENING
Myths
and Misconceptions

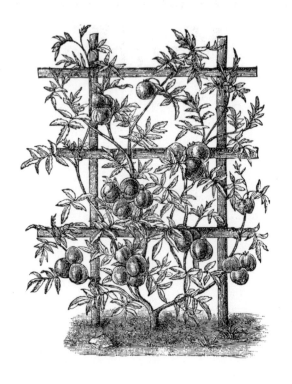

GARDENING
Myths

and Misconceptions

CHARLES DOWDING

green books

First published in 2014 by
Green Books
PO Box 145, Cambridge CB4 1GQ, England
www.greenbooks.co.uk
+44 1223 302 041

Green Books is an imprint of UIT Cambridge Ltd

Design by Jayne Jones

Front cover main image: Jennifer Johnson

ISBN: 9780857842046 (hardback)
ISBN: 9780857842060 (ePub)
ISBN: 9780857842053 (PDF)
Also available for Kindle

10 9 8 7 6 5 4 3

CONTENTS

To Amanda Cuthbert, with whom I first discussed this
'myths' idea in 2008: she was supportive and encouraged
me to wait until the time was right, which is now!

ACKNOWLEDGEMENTS

I am grateful to Michael and Joy Michaud of Sea Spring Seeds,
professional growers and breeders of chillies, including the Dorset
Naga, for sharing the first four myths given on pages 50-51 ('Some
more choice myths'). They have checked those claims and found
them all to be untrue.

This book, although more modest in size than my others, needed
more careful editing, and I thank Alethea Doran, who has also
done sterling work on my other titles and especially *How to Grow
Winter Vegetables*, for her helpful approach.

Thanks to Stephanie Hafferty for her warmth and support, and for
sharing the humour of myths.

AUTHOR'S NOTE

The external sources indicated with superscript numbers throughout
this book provide further information and can be read online at
www.greenbooks.co.uk/gardening-myths-references/

INTRODUCTION

"It is by no means an irrational fancy that, in a future existence, we shall look upon what we think our present existence, as a dream." **Edgar Allan Poe**

Myths abound. They can be a confusion of language, an evolution towards truth, or simply a collection of misunderstandings that have, by force of widespread repetition, morphed into accepted facts. Most of the myths in this book are of the last kind, yet many also contain an element of ritual, and some embody advice that has become revered to the point that any questioning causes anxieties.

❧

Myths may be more involved in your garden than you realize, and by 'myths' I mean beliefs that are misleading and create unnecessary work. The myths covered in these pages come in varying degrees of certitude: many are believed by almost everyone, and some are partly true, but most are not – in my and others' experience, and in the light of some quoted studies. The choice of myths in this book reflects my own experience of practices that I have found to be misguided, and does not include even more pieces of gardening 'wisdom' that others would describe as mythical.

Many myths are steeped in tradition, or appear to be, and this gives them credence. Others are less traditional but widely accepted, and sound right until you look at the evidence. A good example is the advice that plants should not be watered in bright sunlight, because of the sun scorching their leaves as it shines through water droplets. So frequently is this said that surely it must be true!

Actually in 2009 a team of researchers checked this claim, using computer modelling as well as tests on leaves, and they found that water droplets on a leaf surface were not able to focus the sun's energy for long or powerfully enough to damage the leaves before the water evaporated (see Chapter 3, page 32). I found this reassuring, because for 30 years, when seeing plants in need of moisture, I have always watered in bright sunlight, to reduce leaf wilt on fast-growing plants such as cucumbers and to give water to the small volume of compost in trays. This has kept plants happy in sunny weather and has had another benefit, removing the need to shade my greenhouses – another recommended job.

THE COURAGE TO QUESTION

Most of us feel safer doing things in accepted ways, whatever they are, without always understanding the reasons, and we tend to be suspicious of changes. How can one be sure that a 'new idea' is valid, especially if the old one is apparently working? First you must dare to ask the question and doubt what you have been told, then assess the evidence and compare the advice, perhaps conduct your own experiments, and decide for yourself.

I have a questioning nature, and most of the advice in this book is based on my own experience of what has worked well in my gardens, season after season. I have grown vegetables commercially for 30 years in different soils and in varied locations, tried many ways of growing during that time, and have developed my own simple methods for achieving abundance. My wish is that the advice in these pages can help you, the reader, feel creative in your garden – less constricted by apparent rules; more free to find your own, preferred way of gardening.

I have wanted to write this book for a few years, and now the opportunity has come I must acknowledge a dilemma. In wanting to save the reader from unnecessary jobs and expense, I intend no criticism of those advocating the other accepted ways of gardening that I question here, and I apologise in advance if I offend anyone!

WHERE DO MYTHS COME FROM?

The origins of myths are often difficult to trace, and some have more than one source. For example, a general belief, until around two hundred years ago, that *tomatoes are poisonous* may have originated, in Britain at least,

from the use of pewter plates by wealthier people: the acid of tomatoes caused some of the lead from the pewter to leach into food, making it poisonous. Poor people ate off wooden plates and apparently ate tomatoes without any worries.

❧

Another factor in the power of this myth was the influential John Gerard writing in his 1597 *Herbal* that tomatoes were poisonous, and this claim was mostly accepted until the early 1800s. However, in the United States this changed from 1820, when Colonel Johnson ate a basketful of tomatoes outside a courthouse in New Jersey, in a well-publicized event before 2,000 people: while he ate, the local firemen played a funeral tune to help him die peacefully, until noticing his continued health. Sometimes it takes a dramatic event to correct mistaken beliefs!

SOME MISLEADING HISTORIES

History does not always help clarify things, because it is being continuously rewritten: just look at all the different versions of Shakespeare's life and the ongoing question of whether he wrote the works that bear his name. There are some striking examples of widely held but inaccurate beliefs about people and events. The following are just a few.

Most evidence points to Robin Hood (if he even existed) being a Yorkshire yeoman, but a few medieval ballads linked him to the famously evil sheriff of Nottingham, and then he became firmly established as an ex-aristocrat in Sherwood Forest when Walter Scott's 1820 novel *Ivanhoe* was the first of many tales to put him there.

❧

Marie Antoinette did not, it seems, say "Let them eat cake": this is actually attributed to Louis XIV's wife Maria Theresa, 50 years earlier. The phrase first appears in print in Jean-Jacques Rousseau's *Confessions*, completed in 1769 when Marie Antoinette was a 14-year-old girl in Austria, a full 20 years before the French Revolution.

❧

In Britain, Walter Raleigh is thought to have introduced tobacco and potatoes to Europe, on his return from the Americas in 1586. In fact, tobacco had arrived before

then from France, where it had been introduced in 1560 by Jean Nicot (hence 'nicotine'), and potatoes were growing in Italy by 1585.

❧

Apparently Cinderella wore 'glass' slippers, but the story of Cinderella was popularized in 1697 by the French author Charles Perrault, who elaborated it from old tales where Cinderella wore slippers made of 'vair', which is a medieval word for white squirrel fur, not used in Perrault's time, and he presumably read it as '*verre*', which means 'glass' in French.

❧

Mussolini is 'known' to have 'made the trains run on time', but he achieved it mainly by banning any reporting of the delays, as revealed by the journalist Alexander Cockburn.

FROM MYTH TO 'FACT'

When generally believed, almost any statement can mutate into an accepted fact: for instance, that you must knead dough to make good bread – everybody knows that! However, the baker and food writer Dan Lepard, with some of his course participants, experimented by making batches of dough with and without kneading, then reported being unable to see a difference between their finished loaves – in fact, if anything, the unkneaded dough rose faster! He concluded: "If you want to knead your dough it won't harm it, but it won't help it either."[1]

Certain myths are founded on the common assumption that in today's world of science we understand and can explain how nature works. But history reveals how our scientific understandings change all the time – and yet somehow they are always right.

Here is one example from soil science. For much of the last century, humic acid was believed to contain most of the soil's store of carbon. Then in 1996 the soil scientist Sara Wright discovered a previously unknown substance in soil, named glomalin, which is currently thought to contain a "third of the world's stored soil carbon".[2] Until, that is, the next new discovery.

Whatever the origins of myths, one thing is common to them all. When a belief becomes generally accepted, it takes root and grows in certainty, to the point where questioning it invites ridicule, even when it embodies clear contradictions. There are many such beliefs in gardening, some with discernible origins in history, and some that have established for no obvious reason.

I hope you may laugh at much of the myth-busting in these pages – and question my claims too, because nobody has all the answers. But I also hope that your garden grows better as a result: mine does!

CHAPTER 1

A WEB OF MYTHS AND MISCONCEPTIONS

Gardening myths link together and support each other, establishing a network of jobs that one is supposed to do, and a number of things that one is not supposed to do. Therefore I find that not doing one supposedly necessary job frees me up from needing to do another. This book, then, seeks to unravel a long trail of gardening mysteries and complexities, revealing an underlying simplicity that makes our tasks quicker and less numerous.

❧

You may wonder why some or even much of the advice in this book appears to contradict what you have previously heard – and so do I! I think a lot of confusions arise from the widespread application of good knowledge in the wrong place, and there are several reasons why this has happened, and continues to happen. Advice may have been valid once and then become inappropriate in changed circumstances; or is based on a translation of inappropriate methods from farming to gardening; or has simply mutated through language, with words being misunderstood.

SOME WELL-ROOTED MYTHS

To give you an idea of how myths grow, here are just three examples of gardening methods that were or are appropriate in their original time or context. They need understanding in that context to see whether they are relevant now or in different settings.

- ❦ In large gardens, owned by wealthy elites, there was spare labour in winter for jobs such as washing pots (to restrict the spread of disease) and digging soil (for all the commonly cited reasons), with no need to ask how necessary these jobs are.
- ❦ Many mixed farms, at least until the advent of chemical fertilizers and weedkillers, practised an average four-year rotation of crops – which makes sense in large fields where the same plants are grown in large blocks and animals are available to graze pasture. However, in gardens, especially small gardens and also where double-cropping is practised in the same year, a four-year rotation is often impractical and restricts the output of produce.
- ❦ The use of undecomposed mulches, while good for protecting the soil surface in dry climates, causes problems in damp climates, where there is less need to conserve moisture at all times, because the mulches provide habitat for slugs.

REALLY? WHY IS THAT SO?

Many questions I am asked about tips for better gardening start with something along the lines of 'My allotment neighbour / favourite TV presenter said. . .'; 'My mother/uncle advised. . .'; 'I heard/read that. . .' Often the advice sounds highly doubtful to me, but the listener trusts his or her source and does not have enough experience to perceive the unspoken assumptions, hidden misunderstandings and occasional nonsense. If you receive information in this way, and are unsure of its truth, I suggest you reply with a question of your own: 'Why is that so?'

Much freely given advice is not wrong in itself, just inapplicable in all situations. For example: that you 'must have a four-year rotation', 'must water in the evening', 'must run your rows north–south', 'must stake all newly planted trees' and 'must make a trench for growing climbing beans'. All can be answered with: 'Have you ever tried *not* doing any of these things to check how necessary they are?' I know from experience that none of these pieces of advice are rules that have to be followed.

The important thing is to understand why the supposedly necessary task is recommended, so that you are empowered to make your own decision in your particular garden – and thereby be freed from the clutches of rules and recommendations of variable worth. The following examples show how commonly held but inaccurate beliefs are to be found in almost every aspect of gardening.

FEEDING MYTHS

In the last 150 years, new fertilizers made from water-soluble nutrients have completely changed the way that plants are fed. But this has happened without all the understanding necessary to accompany such a radical change of method.

For example, some farmers and gardeners still use the traditional word 'manure', originally a description of nutrient-rich excrements and bedding, as a term for synthetic, water-soluble fertilizers.

Because these fertilizers make soil more acidic over time, this has led, by association with the word 'manure', to a belief that *animal* manures make soil more acidic when used regularly. Many gardeners are confused by this, as I know from frequently being asked to clarify this matter!

More confusion arises when unspoken assumptions about feeding plants are applied to these two fundamentally different approaches. Most of the nutrients in synthetic fertilizers are water-soluble, while the nutrients in composts and composted manures are insoluble in water and become available to plants when tempera-ture and soil biology combine to allow access by growing roots. In practical terms, this means that compost feeds the soil rather than the plants and that you can spread it in autumn, unlike synthetic fertilizer, which would leach away in winter rains. Even some organic gardeners do not appreciate this. See Chapter 7 for more on feeding.

MYTHS AND MISUNDERSTANDINGS ABOUT EQUIPMENT

It is easy to spend money, then frustrating sometimes to discover a simpler approach for less expense. Save your money until you're sure of what you really need for your garden! For example, when growing vegetables we are often encouraged to invest in raised beds with wooden sides. These have some advantages, but check the evidence described on page 38 before you spend the money. Compost-ing can be made expensive too, as I know from spending over £300 on an 'easy turn' tumbler. Well, it was easy to turn, but did not make good compost in the advertised time, even when I was precise about the ingredients added, which is actually quite difficult in gardening. So I continue to make lovely, slow compost in slightly ramshackle, home-made heaps, which cost only my time to assemble and give me more satisfaction. For general gardening tools,

I suggest borrowing or buying a friend's or second-hand ones before investing too much, because we all have different ways of using spades, hoes, trowels and secateurs; no tools are 'best' – only you can decide, based on your own way of using them.

MYTHS ABOUT DE-LEAFING

There are common misconceptions about plant growth, such as the oft-quoted maxim that stripping tomatoes of their leaves in late summer helps fruit to ripen. Some extra colour is the most you can achieve by doing this, whereas true ripening is part of the *growing* process, so requires photosynthesis, not just sun hitting the fruit – and ripening fruits need the sugars and nutrients from many (not all) leaves to help them develop the best texture, size and flavour. I suggest removing only the old, lower leaves, which also reduces the risk of blight by increasing the passage of dry air at surface level (more on this on page 41).

It is the same for vines, whose leaves are photosynthesizing in late summer to make sucrose for ripening grapes. They can be partially de-leafed to increase grape colour and above all to improve plant health, by increasing air circulation around the grapes to reduce powdery mildew and rotting of dense bunches. But many leaves are left on vines at this time, to enhance grape sugars and flavours.

There is also a recommendation to remove the fading lower leaves of celeriac, when roots are swelling in late summer and autumn. This certainly makes the plants look more attractive, but when I experimented by removing lower leaves on just one side of a celeriac bed from August onwards, the resulting roots were 20 per cent smaller by November than the untouched celeriac on the bed's other side.

MYTHS ABOUT LOOSE SOIL

One of the biggest misunderstandings within gardening lore is a belief in the value of loosening soil before sowing and planting, and sometimes around existing plants in herbaceous borders. I don't wish to deprive those who enjoy digging and tilling of their pleasure, but seek to reassure those who have been told that loosening soil is necessary, yet don't want to or are unable to. Apart from planting trees and digging out woody roots and parsnips, I disturb soil very little and have found that growth is abundant, with fewer weeds, less need to water and often less slug damage.

Another benefit of this approach is that undisturbed soil is less sticky. In one year of endless rain throughout summer and autumn, I was able to carry on picking, planting and clearing in almost any weather, on an acre of clay soil. While fellow growers were mired in mud, my land was full of new plantings, with fewer weeds and less slug damage than is 'normal' in such weather.

MYTHS ABOUT SLUGS

Except in extreme weather, slugs do not randomly eat any old (or young) plant, because their role is to *recycle* decaying and weak leaves. Growing plants in well-fed soil and keeping slug habitat to a minimum reduces damage, although vigilance is always required.

I have found in my dig/no-dig experiment that there is less slug damage in the undug beds than in the dug beds growing the same plants. There are probably the same number of slugs in each case, but the crucial point is that when plants are *healthier*, slugs eat less of them, and this is just one part of an interconnected sequence of cause and effect in untilled soil:

- Fewer weeds germinate because undisturbed soil has most of its weed seeds lying dormant at depth, away from the light, which would trigger their germination.
- Fewer weeds results in less habitat of their moist leaves for slugs to hide in by day and then eat by night.

❦ Compost on top has a rougher surface than dug soil of most types and especially silts and clays; slugs prefer soft soil for slithering over, and appear somewhat less active on surface compost.

All the examples in this chapter illustrate the interconnected nature of gardening practice, both for better and for worse. They show how understanding myths and being released from their tyranny can free up our time, enable better growth for our crops and make our gardening more creative.

CHAPTER 2

SOWING AND PLANTING

Some well-known pieces of advice about raising plants, which may have been sensible in their original context, have turned into misleading myths. Seeds want to grow, and when sowings are timed to give them the correct temperature, you need worry less about having a perfect seedbed or clean seed trays.

'Vegetable seeds should be sown in spring.'
Partly true

Gardeners worry, and are led to worry by those who have sown early, that seeds must all be in the ground at the first hint of spring. This is untrue, because for best results there are different times of sowing for different vegetables, from February to November. In fact, a great tip is to be patient in spring, since later sowings of heat-loving plants often catch up earlier ones. Be ready with different seed at all times, in order to keep the plot full and have harvests in every month. Here are some guideline dates for sowing vegetables outdoors:

- Early or late winter: broad beans.
- Early spring: peas, spinach, lettuce, parsnips, onions, early potatoes, calabrese and carrots.

- Mid-spring: maincrop potatoes, beetroot, leeks, autumn cabbage.
- Late spring: chard, Brussels sprouts, squashes, courgettes, French and runner beans, swedes.
- Early summer: cucumbers, carrots and beetroot for winter, kale, Savoy cabbage, lettuce for summer.
- Midsummer: chicory for radicchio, coriander, chervil, wild rocket.
- Late summer: salad rocket, oriental leaves, endive, spinach for winter, spring cabbage and onions.
- Early autumn: wide range of salad for winter leaves.
- Mid-autumn: garlic.

'Pots and trays for seeds and plants must be clean and sterile.' *Untrue*

Washing and sterilizing containers is a long and unexciting job, so it is good that even the Royal Horticultural Society is now agreeing that it is not a necessary task after all. Perhaps historically it had become a habitual task in large gardens, where pot washing was something to keep spare labour occupied in winter months, and other gardeners then copied their supposed superiors. Common diseases of plant raising are avoidable with good practice and do not originate in the materials used.

For raising and growing vegetable plants, I never even brush or clean any of my trays and pots between uses, let alone sterilize them: over three decades they have produced up to a hundred batches of healthy plants, with trays being used three or four times a year, simply refilled with new compost for each sowing. The occasional diseases I have experienced are results of the weather and my mistakes – mainly damping off (leaves killed by fungi) in humid conditions when seedling leaves were too close together, watered too often or sowed too early.

'Plants grown under cover always need careful hardening off before planting in soil.' *Partly true*

'Hardening off' means keeping indoor-raised plants outside for a day or two before planting them in soil. Some hardening off is good; however, as with many statements that have become rules, this needs to be qualified, and there are cases where hardening off can be avoided to save time and speed up growth. I know this from success-ful plantings of lettuce, spinach, beetroot, onions, courgettes, peas and so forth, brought out of the greenhouse and put in the soil straight away. In spring, when the air is cold but the sun is bright, I use fleece to cover new plantings, so that although the plants' roots are briefly cooler than they were used to, their leaves are protected from wind, which is often more harmful than low temperatures.

Also, you need to know which plants are frost-hardy, because one often encounters advice such as 'cover broad beans, peas, sweet peas and garlic plants to keep frost off, or bring them back indoors at night'. Yet none of those plants are killed by frost – and nor are lettuce, spinach, brassicas or onions. Only cucurbits, tomatoes, summer beans and sweetcorn are killed by freezing, so wait until frosts are finished before planting them out.

❧

'Soil is best pre-warmed by covering before sowing and planting.' *Untrue*

I have tried this and noticed little difference – certainly not com-pared with the more important job of covering *after* sowing and planting, when growth is actually happening. Pre-warmed soil does not hold on to that extra heat for long, and plants benefit more from being protected once they are in place: not only having some extra warmth but also with less wind blowing their leaves.

Warmer soil in spring is something to strive for, and when I was member of a growers' cooperative in the 1980s, the other growers always commented on the earliness of my crops. This set me wondering whether untilled soil stays warmer for plant growth because there is better conductivity of warmth from deeper below ground. When soil has been tilled, a 'dividing line' is created between denser, homogeneous soil below and the looser, tilled soil above, making it harder for roots to access moisture at deeper levels, and this probably also interrupts the rise of warmth from below.

❧

'You cannot transplant root vegetables.' *Untrue*

Root vegetables can all be transplanted, but special care is needed with carrots and parsnips to preserve the main taproot in one piece before planting. This can be done either by planting them small or by using long 'plugs', such as toilet rolls or root-trainers. All other root vegetables transplant easily, especially when started off in modules to ensure reliable germination, minimal root disturbance and to bring the harvest forwards. For example, you can sow beetroot under cover in late winter for planting a month later under fleece, harvesting them before midsummer when their flavour is especially sweet and other vegetables are scarce.

To save space, time and compost, sow four seeds of beetroot, shallot or radish, or up to six seeds of onion, in the same module and plant them out as a clump, with the developing roots then swelling together and outwards in their clump. Sow two swede seeds in a module and thin to the strongest, for growing into one large root from a planting in early summer. The tiny seeds of celeriac are best sown in a seed tray for pricking into modules when seedlings have two leaves, then planted out before early summer.

'Certain other plants need to be sown direct.'
Often untrue

Although similar to the previous myth, this one is more vague, but one sees advice such as 'coriander / Californian poppy / etc. are best sown direct because they do not like being transplanted'. Well, judging by how well they have grown for me after being transplanted, I take such statements with a pinch of salt. Often I transplant twice: pricking out from seed tray to module, followed by planting out into soil.

A belief such as this may derive from poor growth for reasons other than transplanting, such as inferior potting compost, unfavourable growing conditions or poor soil. Once you have a propagating space and some trays and compost, you can save time and money by raising plants in controlled conditions rather than sowing direct, especially from using fewer expensive seeds. Also, while seeds are germinating and growing in trays, you have more time to clear weeds and make sure the soil is ready before planting out. Out of the wide range of vegetables and flowers I grow, the only seeds I sow direct are carrots, parsnips and occasionally others, such as spinach and lamb's lettuce (corn salad), if I am growing a large amount.

❧

'Soil must be as fine as possible for sowing seeds.' *Often untrue*

All tools, especially power tools, give us the ability to knock soil around more than is good, and I have seen many problems arising from seedbeds made too fine, where soil has been pulverized by machines, or even just run through with a rake, to the point of losing its inherent crumb structure. Sometimes this results in a thin, hard crust on top – a phenomenon known as capping – which in dry weather prevents germinated seeds from sending their first leaves upwards, causing them to perish, even though their roots were developing.

Capping is unlikely in sand and chalk soils, and also where plenty of organic matter is near or on the surface, because compost stays aerated and slightly aggregated together, even after being raked to a tilth for sowing. I find it soft to sow into, with its larger lumps helping to keep the surface open.

Germination and growth is helped most by the structure around developing roots being firm yet aerated, which is always the case in undug, surface-composted soil. This means that one can sow at the appropriate time of year with little preparation needed, and with small lumps in the seed drill.

❧

'Seeds need sowing at particular spacings for each vegetable.' *Often untrue*

While it is important to give seedlings enough space, and this varies for each vegetable – there is no absolute correct spacing, because it depends on how large you want plants to grow before harvest, and how quickly. Closer spacings mean quicker harvests of smaller leaves and roots, such as produced when thinning carrots and spinach. In fact, thinning is not necessary when sowing is precise: for example, beetroot and onions grow well in clumps of four or five roots. This saves compost and space when raising plants, and can increase yields too, with fewer large roots and more medium-sized ones, according to how you sow and grow. Also, if your soil is fertile, spacings can be closer, which also helps to shade out weed growth. Use the spacings on seed packets as guidelines rather than rules.

Another tip is to space all vegetables for salad leaves at 15-22cm (6-9"), according to the leaf size you want. This applies to lettuce, endive, spinach, chard, kale, pea shoots, oriental leaves, land cress, rocket and herbs. It keeps things simple and makes it quicker to sow and plant many different vegetables together, with no need to look up a particular spacing for each.

'There are precise dates for sowing according to the moon.'

Partly true

Now, I believe in lunar forces having an influence on sowing dates, but I include this as a myth because of the difficulty in isolating which moon changes are most important. For example, Maria Thun's influential sowing calendar works mostly with astrological signs and pays little attention to whether the moon is waxing or waning, yet many older farmers use that to guide their sowings, while French farmers I knew paid strict attention to whether the moon was ascending or descending.

Experiments I have made with sowing carrots on slightly different dates according to waxing, waning and astrological signs have given strongly different results at certain times of year, but less so at others, indicating that moon changes have more influence on sowings in spring than in summer.

Partly it depends on whether you want simply the highest yield or whether your aim is to encourage or discourage one aspect of plants' growth – for example, to have carrots with more root and less leaf, sow when the moon is in an 'Earth' sign. Or to encourage vigorous growth, sowing two days before full moon is good when possible. To influence the balance of growth, Maria Thun's approach is worth checking out.

CHAPTER 3

WATERING

There is enough mythology around watering to have made a simple job seem complicated. Debunking the myths makes it easier to see ways of achieving healthy growth, such as watering in the morning, and watering in bright sunlight if plants need it.

'Water in the evening so that less moisture is lost to evaporation.' *Often untrue*

Watering plants is such a key part of gardening and is worth understanding well, to achieve consistent and healthier growth. Clearing up some of the many misconceptions about watering is a good starting point, and this myth about the right time of day for watering is widely believed.

Indeed there is less evaporation in the night than in the day, so leaves and soil stay wet for longer, but is this water 'hanging around' at night actually a good thing for plants? I find that moisture at night makes it easier for slugs to slither around and for fungal diseases such as mildew to develop. By contrast, morning watering is soon dry on both leaves and the soil or compost surface, resulting in a lower incidence of pests and diseases, while the soil stays moist underneath.

A key part of this is what one means by 'watering', and I mean being thorough, giving enough water to soak in and last as long as is possible and practical. For pots and modules in fine weather, water thoroughly so they are close to full capacity, giving roots a reserve of moisture underneath what will be a drying surface. For beds of soil and compost, water sufficiently that plants have enough for a few days' growth, so the surface is dry for longer. See below for more watering tips.

WATERING TIPS

Watering is easier to get right when the soil has a reasonable amount of organic matter – at least 5 per cent and preferably more than that for vegetables, because organic matter is sponge-like, with more ability than soil to hold on to moisture.

❧

The kind of watering to avoid is sprinkling small amounts on a regular basis, which certainly does result in high losses from evaporation, and is less healthy for plants. I suggest you check dry-looking soil with a trowel *before* watering, just to see how much moisture is present underneath: in clay soils there may be more than you think.

❧

You could also sometimes check the soil *after* watering: scrape the surface with a trowel to see how far the moisture has penetrated. If soil was really dry before watering, you may be surprised how dry it still is! This is because some water runs through dry soil until it has swelled up with moisture, so you need to water more gradually. Fortunately, most plants can survive amazingly well in dry soil and pots, with just a maintenance ration, then they grow fast when more water is provided.

'Small seedlings are best watered from below and not from above.' *Often untrue*

When discussing watering with students on my gardening courses, I am amazed at the things they have been advised to do. This particular myth leads to the unnecessary use of capillary matting, the purpose of which is to hold moisture underneath modules and containers, for roots to suck up as they need it. However, I once saw a large propagation area where many seedlings were suffering from a lack of water, either because they had been placed on the damp mat before their still-short roots could contact its moisture, or because the compost was not in contact with the mat. By contrast, when water is applied from above, you can see where more or less water is needed, and watering by hand (use a watering can with a fine rose) enables you to correct any imbalances.

A variation of this myth is that watering from above causes nutrients to leach away, but that could happen only with regular over-watering, and if you are worried about leaching I suggest using organic composts, which hold most nutrients in water-insoluble form (see Chapter 8 for more about compost).

A further myth is that you should use water at the same temperature as your plants, but when you water in the morning, with soil and compost about to warm up during the day, this becomes less important. Do keep a can of water in the greenhouse, but sometimes you will need to use water from the colder water butt outside or from the mains supply.

❧

'Plants in containers need stones, gravel or pottery shards at the bottom to help drainage.' *Untrue*

This is still common practice, despite being demonstrated both theoretically and practically to restrict growth. Water in compost sits between all the small particles, and their large surface area allows a lot of moisture to be retained after watering. But this volume of water also creates enough surface tension that it 'clings' there when it meets the layer of gravel, charcoal or shards you put in the bottom. So these materials actually impede drainage and may cause a waterlogged area above them.

This myth has another bad effect, which is that the container is holding less compost, which means less nutrient content. The smaller volume makes it even harder to give enough water without waterlogging.

A different process can occur in cultivated soils, with potentially similar results, where the tilled zone of soil pieces sits above a dense zone of homogeneous soil: even if there is no 'hard pan' – a compacted layer of soil – the flow of moisture both up and down may be impeded (see page 24, in 'Soil is best pre-warmed by covering before sowing and planting').

❦

'Watering needs doing daily.' *Often untrue*

This is true only for plants whose roots are filling all the compost in a restricted space, be it module, container or growbag, where the limited volume of compost means there is enough water for only a day or two. Pay attention to the weather forecast, because in humid and cooler weather, plants use much less water than in bright sunlight and warm air. Then go steady when plants are maturing their fruits, for example in late summer when you want tomatoes to ripen rather than new fruits to develop (see Chapter 5 for more about tomatoes).

Automatic watering systems for containers can give a certain peace of mind and freedom to leave plants unattended, but they waste more water and are not always so kind to plants, which may be under the stress of too much or too little water. Wherever possible, water by hand, with variable amounts according to the weather and your observation of each plant's needs.

Related to this myth is the common idea that watering is needed when the surface looks dry. This is more likely correct for containers than for soil, where huge reserves are often available to plants at levels we cannot see.

❧

'Watering in sunlight damages leaves.' *Untrue*

This myth has a firm following, yet nobody I know has ever noticed any 'leaf burn' from watering in bright sunlight; nor in fact have any researchers. Dr Gábor Horváth, who led an experiment at Eötvös University in Budapest, Hungary, in 2009, said: "This problem has been dealt with only by amateurs, gardeners and laymen, who could only speculate about this subject. The consequence is that myths rule." The Hungarian physicists checked the results of watering in sunlight, and used computer modelling too, with no findings of any leaf damage. There were just a few deposits on leaves from water impurities, which might be mistaken for damage.[3]

As a control for their experiments, the researchers put glass beads on leaves, which did indeed result in scorching effects, making the point that it is possible to cause leaf scorch through focusing of light, although not by water droplets. This is because water droplets disperse and evaporate before damage occurs, and are too close to the leaf surface for any damage by magnification. This makes sense, since otherwise, in showery weather when the sun is suddenly bright, sometimes even as rain is falling, the harm would be immense!

I find this knowledge really useful for several reasons:

❧ Seedlings and small plants in trays and modules sometimes run out of moisture by afternoon on a hot day, and can be watered in the sunshine with enough water to fully moisten the compost.

- Large plants with a high water content can be helped to get through a day of intense and hot sunlight. This is particularly the case with fast-growing cucumbers, which often perk up when watered like this after struggling to find enough water via their roots, since they can absorb it instead through stomata on their leaves, which then change from being wilted to a normal, fleshy state. It takes only a little water to effect this change, so is highly efficient.
- As a result of the above, there is less need to perform another mostly unnecessary task, namely . . .

❦

'Greenhouses need limewashing or shading before bright summer sun makes them too hot.'
Often untrue

However professional it may look to have a shaded structure, I think you are more likely to reduce growth in this way than increase it, especially in a rather cloudy climate such as Britain's. When I grew vegetables in polytunnels in south-west France, with outdoor temperatures of 36°C (97°F), I found that my plants coped well with days of intense sunlight. Light is key to plant growth: the huge greenhouses at Thanet in the UK have a special glass with low iron content, to allow more light through, and particularly thin glazing bars.

Inadequate ventilation is more likely to be a problem than high light levels, especially in greenhouses, where top lights allow less movement of air than a second door would. Only on a few intensely hot and bright days do well-ventilated plants struggle with the heat, and then some watering at midday (see previous myth) *is* a great boon, especially for fleshy leaved cucurbits and plants with a limited root run. Tall plants may also struggle as they reach the hotter air near the top of the greenhouse – so, in addition to providing sufficient water, be sure to ventilate as much as you can.

CHAPTER 4

VEGETABLE GARDEN PLANNING AND DESIGN

Theories about vegetable garden planning come with their own well-established misconceptions. Understanding them for what they are enables you to be more relaxed in your design and planting schemes – for example, growing what you like instead of what the 'rules' of a vegetable rotation say you ought to grow.

'Crop rotation is important for improving soil fertility.' *Often untrue*

The most-stated rule of crop rotation is that a gap of four years is needed between plants of the same family. This dates back 300 years to a system of rotation invented by Charles 'Turnip' Townshend on his Norfolk estates, where he replaced a fallow year in the traditional three-year rotation with fertility-building clover, and then added turnips to make it a four-year rotation. Both the clover and turnips were food for animals, whose droppings and manure added fertility. This practice was soon widely adopted, and productivity increased for many farmers, until the advent of synthetic nitrogen fertilizer diminished the need for clover and animal manure.

This piece of history is a good illustration of how rules for modern growing and gardening are often rooted in a historical context that may not have relevance today, or may apply only to farm-scale growing but not to gardens, where different methods are used. Garden plots are unlike Townshend's fields, where farmers had little access to compost and were growing larger blocks of the same species.

The most difficult part of any rotation is growing under cover, and this leads to an interesting point about tomatoes – see overleaf.

DIFFICULTIES WITH ADHERING TO A STRICT CROP ROTATION

Part of the rationale for rotation is that it helps to avoid a build-up of soil problems of particular plant families, by growing each family in a different place each year. However, this apparently sound principle is less simple in practice, for various reasons:

❧ It is unlikely that what you want to eat, and end up planting, will match the precisely defined quotas of a specific rotation.
❧ In a small garden, many vegetables of different rotational families are cheek-by-jowl, and disease problems could occur where they meet the edges (although they often don't).
❧ Many vegetables grow in half a season, so unless you sow and plant the same vegetable again in summer when your first harvest is cleared, which seems to contradict the principle of rotation, you will effectively be growing two years' cropping in one year, in terms of plant families, so a four-year rotation has to become a two- or three-year rotation.

Four-year gaps are difficult, and I suggest two years or more between vegetables of each main family, depending on which you grow the most of. The main groupings to consider are brassicas, legumes, umbellifers (carrots, etc.), Cucurbitaceae, chenopods (beets), Solanaceae (potatoes, etc.), plus miscellanies including many salads.

'You must change the soil of a greenhouse each year to keep growing tomatoes.' *Partly true*

There is sound theory behind this myth, as soil pests that harm the roots of tomato plants do build up. But in practice it is a big undertaking and has resulted in gardeners either using growbags instead of their greenhouse soil or doing a lot of soil moving in the name of soil hygiene. Changing the soil every year is a lot of work, but there are other options: you can add lots of new compost, and alternate tomato crops with melons, cucumbers and other exotic vegetables, for example.

I grow good tomatoes every second year by adding three inches of my best compost or 12-to-18-month-old animal manure on top of the soil. This reduces the effects of soil pests, keeps soil healthy and fertile, and ensures a worthwhile yield of tasty fruit. I have seen greenhouses with good tomato crops still after five successive years of growing them. You can also grow abundant winter salads in the same soil, with no extra compost added: sow seeds in modules or trays in early autumn, to plant a month later as soon as the tomatoes are removed.

❧

'You need a plan for creating and maintaining a vegetable garden.' *Partly true*

While an approximate plan is good, it is important to understand that traditions in the laying out and even planting of vegetable plots have been influenced by ornamental gardening, where hard land-scaping and the predominance of perennial plantings make it necessary to start with a precise design. By contrast, in vegetable gardens most of the area is soil and most plants are annuals, so the main planning requirement is to do with the orientation and size of beds, in addition to locating sheds, greenhouses and other structures.

Once you have decided on those few things, it works well to have approximate ideas of where you will sow and plant, rather than defining fixed areas and boundaries, which becomes difficult when you have too few or too many plants, or some plants are eaten by slugs, or a friend offers you some good ones, or you'd like to try growing something new. Gardening is more fun when you can be spontaneous and creative according to your own wishes rather than someone else's prescription, and I find that the fast-changing shape and form of vegetable growing is as exciting as any formal plan or structure.

❦

'You should run beds and rows in a north–south direction.' *Partly true*

As with many myths, a statement with some truth is here given as a rule, although in most situations it is outweighed by more important factors. For one thing, where do you access your garden or plot? The location of the entrance point or gateway is important, to have easy access into pathways and between rows of plants. Sloping ground is a consideration too, since a really steep slope means you can make beds across in a terracing effect, while on a gentle slope it works best to have beds running up and down.

The main reason for a north–south orientation is to prevent tall plants from keeping the midday sun off smaller plants on their north side. However, the chief culprits for causing shade are climbing beans, and the fact is that they grow in summer when there is a lot of morning and evening sunlight from east and west, which diminishes the worry about shading. Most other common vegetables are quite low-growing, no more than 60cm (2') high, thus causing no shade problems. See also the next myth.

'Greenhouses and polytunnels need to be aligned north—south.' *Partly true*

This advice has arisen for two main reasons, both to do with midday sun from the south: to minimize shading of low plants by their tall neighbours, and to reduce heat in hot weather, by having the sun shine on only the short end of a north—south structure rather than on the long side of an east—west structure.

I have always had good growth in polytunnels oriented both ways, in the same garden, and find that growth in winter is stronger in an east—west structure, for the same reason that this orientation is advised against in summer – it captures more of the low midday sun on its long side, rather than on a southern end. And, in most of the UK at least, sunlight is generally too rare and weak to make overheating an issue (see also page 33, 'Greenhouses need lime-washing or shading before bright summer sun makes them too hot').

There are more important considerations in deciding where and how to site a structure: on an exposed plot it is worth orienting the ends with the prevailing wind direction, and the point of access is often a deciding factor, as it's advisable to position door-ways as close as possible to the garden entrance and also to water butts and hoses.

❦

'Raised beds need wooden sides.' *Partly true*

In small plots there is a case for having wooden sides to define beds, but in larger plots, beds can be open-sided and with less definition between bed and path level (see next myth too). This conserves moisture, especially when there is some compost on pathways, because beds have less of an edge for water to evaporate from; and it reduces pests, because wooden sides usually encourage a build-up of slugs, woodlice and ants. I have seen this difference clearly when comparing growth in wooden-sided beds with growth of the same vegetables in beds with no sides.

Wooden sides can cause unforeseen problems: in one wet summer, for example, my celeriac roots in an open-sided bed were 95-per-cent clean, while those in neighbouring wooden-sided beds, although looking good at harvest in November, were full of tunnels made by woodlice. The planks were six-year-old softwood, slightly decayed and offering a home to hordes of these insects: their depredations of plants are often less visible than those of slugs, but can be dramatic, so I suggest you consider all options before edging your beds with wood, and you can save money as well as avoid problems.

❦

'Paths need to be mulched with weed-suppressing materials.' *Partly true*

Paths do need to be weed-free, and an *initial* phase of mulching weeds is often necessary for a year or so. A useful material for clearing path weeds when starting with weedy ground is thick cardboard, sometimes with a little compost, wood shavings or sawdust on top so that you can walk on the paths in wet weather without making holes in the cardboard. Often a second layer of cardboard is needed after two or three months. Then, once the pathway soil is clean, you can mulch with a little compost – nothing else.

Be wary of slug-harbouring materials such as carpet, straw and bark, and remember to continue weeding even if you have paths covered with plastic membrane: just pull out any weeds you see before they can root through the material. It's a good idea to keep paths as narrow as possible: I find that 45cm (18") gives sufficient access, with less maintenance than is needed for wider paths. Vegetables send many roots into pathways when beds have open sides, and the bits of compost which fall off beds, or are flicked off by birds as they hunt for worms, help pathways stay free-draining and nice to walk on.

CHAPTER 5

ANNUAL VEGETABLES

A fair number of the myths relating to particular vegetable crops are about tomatoes and root vegetables, and it is fascinating to discover how many oft-stated maxims are misleading and result in extra work or poorer harvests.

TOMATOES

'Tomatoes must be given liquid feed.' *Partly true*

While this *is* true for tomato plants grown in containers and grow-bags, it is not true for those grown in the ground in healthy soil, where plants can root further and more extensively to find the food they need. Also, this advice is based on a more synthetic than organic view of nutrition, with the implication that soil is an inert medium for holding food. This is not untrue as such, but individual nutrients are only part of what makes healthy growth. For example, potash plays a major role in helping fruits to grow and become plentiful, but only when other elements are in the correct balance. There is a risk, when giving synthetic feeds, of distorting this balance of nutrients.

I grow abundant tomatoes in soil with compost on top and no liquid feeds: the quality and flavour are good, and it is less work! Feeding in summer can become a chore and is best kept for plants with restricted root runs in containers and growbags, for which a plant-based feed, say from the leaves of stinging nettle and comfrey, will save money and promote balanced growth.

❧

'Removing all leaves in late summer helps tomatoes ripen.' *Untrue*

A gardener asked me, in early October, why her tomatoes were dull tasting and of mealy texture – then it emerged that she had followed advice seen on television to remove all leaves to encourage the fruit to ripen. The idea behind this seems to be that 'sun on fruit helps it ripen'. But while sun on fruit can give extra colour (as with grapes – see page 18), it cannot develop the full flavour, sweetness and texture one seeks in ripe fruits. Plants need leaves to photosynthesize, converting solar energy to sugars and other compounds required by fruit as they mature. (A study on the photosynthetic activities of vegetative and fruiting tissues of ripening tomatoes found that leaves account for 71 per cent of photosynthesis, stem tissue 14 per cent and green fruit 15 per cent.[4])

A good approach is to keep removing the lower leaves only, below the bottom truss of fruit, to improve ventilation and help keep blight at bay, but to keep all other leaves. You can encourage tomatoes to ripen by removing the plant's main growing point in high summer, watering less in the final six weeks and pinching out any new side-shoots – all this encourages it to put energy into swelling and ripening the existing fruit, rather than into making new leaves and fruit.

'Grafted plants are worth the extra cost, for bigger harvests.' *Untrue*

Sometimes the harvests from grafted plants are bigger, but not always, and given their cost of around £3 each you are probably better off spending the money on some extra compost. *Which? Gardening* did a trial of grafted and ungrafted tomato plants in 2012 and concluded, in their April 2013 issue, that the small increase in harvest, of around 10 per cent, does not justify the significant expense. (However, they did find a good increase of fruit in a few cases, although noting that the process of grafting checks the growth of plants in spring and may delay harvest a little.)

To find out more, I grew three plants of grafted 'Sweet Million' tomatoes alongside ungrafted ones. The grafted plants grew with exceptional vigour, while the ungrafted ones were smaller and a little yellow and looked less healthy by comparison, presumably owing to soil pests nibbling their roots. However, I harvested fruit earlier from the ungrafted plants and over the season they yielded more, while the grafted plants' trusses of fine tomatoes were slower to ripen – perhaps because of a lack of stress triggers, i.e. the very pests they are designed to overcome.

❧

'You can't grow cucumbers and tomatoes together.' *Untrue*

This myth may have originated in large gardens where there was plenty of greenhouse space to keep the two vegetables separate, as they do indeed prefer slightly different growing regimes. However, they can certainly be grown together, and I always grow them both in the same polytunnel because I do not have the room to keep them apart. Cucumbers like moist air and tomatoes like dry air, but average air is good for both!

Just make sure that ventilation in hot weather is adequate and that your cucumber plants have enough moisture around their roots: on really hot days, they enjoy a sprinkle of water on their leaves around midday, to help them stay moist in bright sunshine (see page 33, in 'Watering in sunlight damages leaves'). Tomatoes should not usually be watered on their leaves, unless aphids need washing off – in early summer mainly. In damp summers, and from mid-summer onwards, you need to keep tomato leaves as dry as possible to reduce the risk of blight, so water plants at soil level only.

ROOT VEGETABLES

'Root vegetables form one part of a crop rotation.' *Untrue*

The term 'root vegetable' is misleading because it embraces plants of many families, whose 'roots' are anything from swollen stems (e.g. kohlrabi) to tubers (e.g. potatoes) to swollen food stores above the plant's main rooting system (e.g. carrots, parsnips, etc.). These plants are categorized together as root vegetables but, being of different families, they all grow in entirely different ways, with different issues of pest and disease. This means that each one is in a separate group for the purposes of working out a crop rotation, if you use one (see page 35).

❧

'Overfed onions are all leaf and no root.' *Partly true*

All plants need leaves to help feed their roots, and the point is really about balance. Occasionally a soil with too much fresh manure, or too much nitrogen fertilizer, could grow onions with more leaf than root, but all plants make bigger harvests when soil is nourished with mature compost and manure. Each ring of onion bulbs comes from one leaf, with larger rings from larger leaves, so fertile soil grows larger onions.

'Roots of beetroot swell below ground.' *Partly true*

Often, while I am teaching students on my gardening courses and we are looking at beetroot growing and swelling above soil level, the same question is asked: 'As a root vegetable, why are they not below ground?' The answer is that the beets we eat happen to be root swellings above the main root system and, apart from a variety called 'Cheltenham Green Top', which grows down into the soil like a fat carrot, they mostly swell up above ground – as do swedes, celeriac, many turnip and radish varieties, onions and kohlrabi. This results in a colour change in the above-ground part, but in most cases this does not affect the flavour or mean that it is harmful to eat (see below).

COLOUR CHANGES OF ROOT VEGETABLES IN LIGHT

Any part of a plant that is exposed to light starts to photosynthesize, and this causes a colour change, as more green – chlorophyll pigment – is added to the existing colour. Look closely at a red beetroot and you can see how the part above ground is browner than the brighter red part below ground, because red and green make brown: this is not a toxic or flavour-spoiling change. Carrots develop green shoulders in daylight unless covered with soil: again, this does not make them harmful to eat, although does give them a slight bitter flavour. Turnip roots go a little green on top where exposed to light, but this is not detrimental to the flavour. However, light on potato tubers causes the development of solanine just under the skin, which is toxic, so any green parts need cutting off before cooking.

'Potatoes cannot grow in undug soil.' *Untrue*

There is a confusion here between potato roots and tubers. Potato plants can root successfully into undisturbed soil, as I see every year on my clay soil, but they need loose soil or compost for their tubers to swell in, and enough of it on top to keep the potatoes white as their tubers push upwards (hence the term 'earthing up'). For decent-sized tubers you need a depth of about 10cm (4") of loose soil or compost on top, which can also be capped with fresher manure, cardboard, grass mowings, old leaves, black poly-thene and anything else to keep light off the tubers.

❦

'Potatoes clean the soil.' *Partly true*

For anybody new to growing potatoes this is a misleading state-ment, because it hides the work and skill involved in tending the soil before and while growing potatoes. Most of the weed-cleaning is effected by soil cultivation or the application of mulches. For example, pulling the soil from around potato plants to earth them up is an effective way of burying many weeds and weed seedlings. An alternative to earthing up is to grow potatoes under a mulch of any combination of other materials, such as manure or straw (see above), which reduces the growth of perennial weeds too. That said, it's true that once potato plants are growing strongly, their leaves do make a thick, light-excluding cover of their own, for as long as they stay healthy and free of blight.

This myth is reminiscent of the claim that 'pigs clean the soil': in this case the part missed out is that they do not root out everything, with docks and brambles often left growing strongly. Also, they can make a mess of the soil structure in wet weather!

OTHER VEGETABLES AND SALADS

'Lettuce is very pH-sensitive and requires a pH of 6.5-6.8.' *Untrue*

I found this statement on a website of an organic grower who produces lovely lettuce, but comments like this can make gardeners worry unnecessarily about being unable to meet the demands of particular plants, and perhaps put them off growing (in this case) lettuce. I know from experience that this advice is wrong. I have always grown abundant lettuce in different gardens, where the pH has ranged from 6.4 to 8.3, and I also grow lettuce in many different combinations of compost, old manure and soil, of varying pH.

Be cautious of any precise numbers in gardening advice, because there are so many variables with growing plants that isolating any one while ignoring all the others often results in wrong advice.

❧

'You need to sow lettuce every two or three weeks to have harvests all the time.' *Untrue*

This myth is more misleading than wrong, because it assumes that you are harvesting lettuce as hearts. If instead you harvest lettuce leaves, the intervals between new sowings can rise to two or three months rather than two or three weeks. Plant out lettuces 22cm (9") apart and never cut across their tops with a knife, so that the small central leaves are not damaged and can grow more quickly. Use finger and thumb to pick outer leaves only, on a regular basis, and plants can keep producing new leaves for up to 12 weeks in spring, before rising to flower.

I produce lettuce continuously from late April to October using just two sowings: the first in February or March and the second in June. I have produced salad bags for over a decade using this method, concentrating on careful picking rather than frequent sowing; never using a knife for harvesting leaves (not 'cut and come again' but 'pick and come again'). For year-round harvests, you want soil rich in organic matter to keep plants healthy; sow in modules in late winter, early summer, midsummer and early autumn, with some protection over winter for the last sowing – more from wind than from frost.

❧

'When planting leeks, water them in but leave the dibbed hole empty of soil.' *Untrue*

There is a shortage of explanation as to why this practice is recommended: one suggestion is that leeks require an empty hole to swell into. I heard this from my mother and she was adamant that it was necessary, but I found that watering new plants like this, especially in dry weather, can cause them to float out of the dibbed hole. And common sense suggests that roots stay more moist if some soil is pushed into the hole when planting, so that is what I have always done and my leek harvests have been good.

An associated myth is that 'leeks must be planted deeply', but it mainly depends on what you like to eat. It is true if you like leek shanks (stems) to be white and extra sweet, but if you are happy with them being pale green, you can plant leeks at surface level like other vegetables, with their stems mostly above ground. However, leeks for winter and spring harvest in cold climates *are* better planted in deep holes or earthed up, to lessen the impact of frost on their stems, which are more vulnerable to extreme cold than their leaves.

'Wait to harvest garlic until all its leaves turn yellow.' *Untrue*

This advice means harvesting garlic bulbs in late summer, by which time their outer skins are often starting to decompose, preparing for the approaching time in autumn when cloves grow again. Therefore, when you want garlic to store well, it is best harvested when its leaves are half green – usually during the month following midsummer's day, depending on the variety, sowing date and spring weather. Garlic maturity is mainly regulated by day length, with new growth almost stopping by the time of the longest day, although some varieties continue swelling their bulbs for another month.

Soon after the summer solstice, scrape some soil away to check that bulbs are swollen, and with cloves just differentiated. Once they are, you can lift them with a trowel, trim off their roots (easier than when the roots have become tough and dry) and hang them up to dry. With an earlier harvest date the bulbs not only store better but also look nicer, and you have more time to grow a second crop of other vegetables in the space vacated.

❧

'Rocket is rocket.' *Untrue*

There is a confusion of words here, or rather a lack of words, because 'salad rocket' and 'wild rocket' are different vegetables, best grown and picked in different ways. Salad rocket (*Eruca sativa*) is biennial; best sown in late summer to make plenty of leaves for picking from autumn through until early spring, before plants flower in the spring. If you sow it in the spring, harvests are small before plants rise to flower.

Wild rocket, on the other hand (*Diplotaxis tenuifolia*, also known as perennial wall rocket), is indeed perennial and grows more slowly from tiny seeds, so is best sown in midsummer for some autumn leaves, before it goes dormant through winter. Then its roots spring back to life in the spring and grow many new leaves for two or three months, giving a strong rocket flavour to dishes long after salad rocket has gone to seed. Wild rocket goes to seed through the summer; it self-seeds prolifically, but if you cut the flowering plants down to their stem ends after flowering, new growth appears by early autumn.

❧

'When removing leguminous plants after final harvest, leave their roots in the soil with all the nitrogen nodules.' *Virtually untrue!*

Most of legumes' nitrogen fixing is done while growing and for their own use, such that only a few of the fertilizing nodules are left after all beans and peas are harvested. On BBC Radio 4's *Gardeners' Question Time*,[5] Chris Beardshaw discussed the results of a study showing that after legumes reach flowering stage, the nitrogen flows from the nodules to the plants, with just 3 per cent of the original nitrogen 'fix' left on roots after the pod harvest. Therefore, to increase soil nitrogen, you need to cut plants' stems when they are still in full leaf, which is not possible if you want to harvest the pods. To benefit a following crop, legumes need to be grown as a green manure only (see page 65).

By the time of final harvests, plants are dying off, with pea leaves going yellow with mildew, broad bean leaves mostly fallen and sometimes diseased with chocolate spot, and runner beans at their season's end. Nonetheless, you can cut stems at soil level to leave roots in the soil, which has the advantage of causing less disturbance to the soil, as well as leaving some nodules of nitrogen for the next planting. Or, if you gently pull plants out with their main root intact, any attached nodules will benefit your compost heap instead.

SOME MORE CHOICE MYTHS

'Growing chillies and sweet peppers together results in mixed flavours.'
Untrue

The supposed problem here is cross-pollination – which, if it influenced the fruits, would indeed lead to quite a medley of flavours. But although cross-pollination by insects does occur with chillies and peppers, in the same way as with squashes and courgettes, it does not affect the first year's fruits. The issue can only arise in the following year, if the plants cross-pollinated and you then use the seeds inside the fruits to grow new plants.

'Runner beans are helped to set fruit by watering plants at flowering stage.' *Untrue*

Favourable weather allowing pollination by insects is the important thing for flowering plants, and that is out of our control. What we can do is grow healthy plants that flower for longer – in soil with plenty of organic matter, giving water at the roots in dry weather.

'Removing all side-shoots from sweetcorn plants results in bigger cobs.' *Untrue*

A French farmer once told me how he side-shooted his whole field of maize, so that seemed reason enough to believe it worth doing, and I did so for a long time until hearing Michael Michaud's* experience of comparing plants with and without side-shoots, which all proved to have similar cobs.

❧

'Cucurbit seeds must be sown on their sides / ends / specific way up or down.' *Untrue*

I used to think it was important to sow these long seeds with the flat end down, which is the end from which roots emerge, but the Michauds* tried sowing batches of seed in all different ways and found no difference in growth. So now I just pop them flat on the surface and cover with a little compost, and growth is good.

❧

'You should pull soil away from onion bulbs to help them swell.' *Untrue*

Soil does not need pulling away from onion bulbs as they swell in summer; they can easily manage this and usually push above soil level anyway, in a similar way to beetroot.

❧

'Lettuce seed won't germinate in high temperatures.' *Partly true*

After making hundreds of lettuce sowings in summer warmth, in a greenhouse, I have found that the main thing to avoid in hot weather is sunshine on the seed tray or soil, and that any kind of shade cover helps seeds to germinate, even in midsummer warmth.

* See Acknowledgements.

CHAPTER 6

TREES, SHRUBS AND PERENNIAL VEGETABLES

This chapter reveals how some generally recommended and widely accepted approaches to gardening tasks, such as how to plant and whether to support new trees, can fall out of favour as understanding develops about better – and often simpler – methods.

TREES AND SHRUBS

'All newly planted trees should be staked.'
Untrue

There are only certain situations in which a tree should be staked, and even then the advice applies to large trees mostly, because staking a small tree can hinder its root development. But it is common advice to stake all trees – probably driven by gardeners' desire to look after plants as much as possible – and I have spent arduous hours driving posts into soil beside newly planted maiden fruit trees. Now I save myself the effort, and the cost of stakes as well. The only times a stake may be needed is when trees are either more than two years old or in full leaf at the time of planting, or are planted on a very windy or steeply sloped site.

Allowing trees to sway in the wind encourages the development of stronger stabilizing roots, whereas staked trees risk staying dependent on this support. When staking is truly necessary, tie the trunk loosely to the stake and aim to remove the support as soon as you are confident that the tree is supporting itself. This advice from Colorado State University's 'Ten Commandments of Tree Planting' in 2010 sums it up nicely: "Trees can be staked too tightly or for too long. Don't stake small trees or those not in the wind's path. Rigid staking of a tree is counterproductive; research shows trees don't develop normally if they're not allowed any sway."[6]

❧

'Add organic matter when filling holes made for planting trees.' *Untrue*

I used to add lots of organic matter when planting trees and bushes, following the advice given to enrich the soil around roots in holes made for planting. But the consensus of advice has now

switched to applying organic matter on the surface – just one of many examples of how misleading myths can suddenly disappear as our understanding improves. Here is some advice from North Carolina State University in 2000:[7]

> Historically, the recommendation was to incorporate organic matter into the backfill (soil used to fill a planting hole). Some gardeners took the practice further and completely replaced the removed soil with purchased topsoil. Research has shown that neither practice helps plants grow and in some cases can be detrimental. When water enters soil with one texture and later comes in contact with soil that has a very different texture, water movement (drainage) is impeded. . . . Some researchers report that amended backfill can cause roots to remain in the planting hole instead of growing into the surrounding soil.

I find that trees grow well from being planted in a hole of native soil, just wide enough for their roots, then mulched with organic matter on top.

❧

'Tree root growth follows the same pattern as the trunk and branches.' *Untrue*

You may have seen lovely artist's impressions of mirror-image growth, suggesting that tree roots go as deep in the soil as their branches grow high. In fact this is rarely, if ever, the case: most tree roots are quite close to the soil surface, where the most moisture can be found and nutrients are recycling. They can also spread out much further horizontally than the crown does, which is an important point to consider when tree planting, especially if you want to grow vegetables nearby.

'You should paint anti-fungal "protector" on new cuts in wood.' *Untrue*

The ends of bare wood after pruning are rapidly colonized by fungal spores, not all of them beneficial, and plants or trees respond with their own defence mechanisms, initially isolating the wounded area to prevent the spread of any infection. But if a gardener applies antiseptic products to new cuts, it can harm organisms in the tree and slow or harm the natural healing process, for example, if moisture is sealed into a wound, favouring some organisms of fungal decay.

It is safest to trust your trees and shrubs to heal themselves, helping them by using sharp secateurs for clean cuts, and by doing your research beforehand on the best times for pruning different types of tree. Trees that make 'stone fruit' (such as plums or peaches) are susceptible to silver leaf fungus on new cuts in winter, so they should always be pruned in early summer, when their fast-flowing sap can seep out of cuts and seal the wounded areas very quickly.

❧

'You should add bonemeal to soil when planting trees and shrubs.' *Untrue*

This myth stems from the knowledge that phosphorus encourages root growth. Bonemeal is indeed rich in phosphorus (and calcium), but few soils are short of these elements, and adding phosphorous to excess serves to slow down the ability of mycorrhizal fungi (see next myth) to penetrate plant roots. When too much phosphorous is present, plant roots cannot secrete the acids that allow mycorrhizae to associate with them, and ironically this has the worst effect at planting time, when roots are working hardest to help plants settle and grow in their new location.

'Adding mycorrhizal formulations to soil helps the establishment of newly planted trees and shrubs.' *Partly true*

Fungi in soil, especially the long filaments of mycorrhizae, are a vital ingredient for healthy plant growth, because without them many nutrients in the soil can lie dormant and unavailable. Most vegetables and all trees and shrubs grow more healthily when their roots can ally with mycorrhizae in the soil to help them access water and nutrients.

However, some research[8] on this claim is *against* the idea of adding packaged fungi to soil, and for one clear and simple reason: if mycorrhizal fungi are lacking in soil, it is because conditions are currently unfavourable to them. Therefore adding fungi to soil is generally a waste of money, although the sellers won't tell you that! Spend your money on some extra organic matter instead. Mycorrhizal fungi, which are mostly invisible to the naked eye, are harmed by lack of organic matter, over-cultivation of soil, poor drainage or too much fertilizer, especially phosphate. Correcting these problems will create the best conditions for your own native mycorrhizae, enabling them to re-grow if their numbers had been reduced, and thereby help all your plants – not just the newly planted ones. This way you will gain all the other benefits of extra organic matter too, such as better moisture retention and drainage, which are helped much less by the addition of a packet of dry powder.

❧

'You need to hand-pollinate apricots (etc.)' *Nearly always untrue*

Hand-pollination is necessary only in unusual and particular situations, such as when saving seed, to be sure the right pollen has fertilized a flower. In terms of fruit production, poor pollination is mostly caused by bad weather conditions, such as a late frost damaging flowers or pro-longed heavy rain at flowering time. The latter can cause irretriev-able damage to flowers by washing out the pollen and nectar, needed for pollination and insect food respectively, so that even if insects do manage to fly on a rare fine day, they will be moving less pollen around simply because it less abundant.

Most at risk from lack of pollinating insects are early-flowering trees such as apricots, whose blossom is out before many insects have emerged. Even so, I have found that in normal weather con-ditions the flowers set well, without any help from me – in fact, I often need to thin the fruit rather than worry about a shortage. This myth about hand-pollination is also often thought to be true of tomatoes. In this case it arises partly from growing tomatoes in greenhouses or polytunnels, where, perhaps, insects are less likely to enter – but again, I have never found this to be a problem.

PERENNIAL VEGETABLES

'Growing perennials is as productive and easier than growing annual/biennial vegetables.'
Partly true

This claim is hotly debated in some circles and is really about the gardener's temperament and how much time he or she has avail-able. For example, quick returns and highest yields through all the seasons are gained mostly from annual sow-ings, but these take more time to look after than perennial plantings. It depends on how you want to garden, and it's worth looking into both approaches to find a balance between them. Perennial vegetables give great harvests in spring, during the 'hungry gap', and annual sowings give more harvests at other times, especially of summer fruits and winter vegetables such as parsnips, onions, squashes, swedes and beetroot.

There are also grey areas in the debate, such as whether potatoes and garlic can be considered to be perennial vegetables (the idea being that you leave a few unharvested to grow again, and need not replant them yourself). In these cases it depends partly on whether you are happy not to rotate plantings (see also page 35), and also, for example, whether you want to face the risk of potato blight from tubers left in soil. Weather is another factor, because a frosty winter can kill potato tubers, whereas a mild winter allows them to re-grow; as with runner beans for that matter (see below), and dahlias in ornamental gardens.

❦

'Runner beans, sweet peppers and tomatoes are perennial plants.' *True but misleading*

This statement is indeed true, but is misleading unless you know these plants' climatic constraints. Perennial vegetables are of two types: they either re-grow every spring from established roots or bulbs which have stored enough energy, or they survive winter as smaller and semi-dormant plants. In both cases success varies with climate, and depends on the severity of winters: if there is enough cold to kill the roots, tubers or stem, a perennial plant in one climatic zone becomes an annual in another. Runner beans are perennial only as long as their tuberous roots are not frozen in winter, so in most of the UK you would need to dig them out before winter and replant in spring. Peppers (including chillies) and tomatoes need a lot of protection to survive winter (as heavily pruned and unhealthy-looking plants) in temperate zones. So, in the UK at least, for all these crops it is easier to start again in spring with fresh seed.

'Seakale and rhubarb need forcing for best results.' *Untrue*

This is not to say that forcing is a bad idea, just that the wrong impression can be given that it is always necessary, and without mentioning how it weakens plants. The choice is yours: either to force plants for sweeter, longer and sometimes earlier stems, or to enjoy rhubarb and seakale unforced, with less damage to the plants' roots. Forcing of any plant, i.e. keeping the light off all leaves, usually with pots, makes stems and leaves paler and sweeter to the taste, but it also means that the leaves cannot photosynthesize and so the roots remain unfed for as long as forcing continues. After harvest and removal of the pot, the plant may need a whole year of normal growth to recover.

I noticed this weakness in plants after forcing seakale for a month, in the belief that it was obligatory, having seen no reference to growing and eating unforced seakale. So now I leave my plants to grow in full light and make regular harvests of the shorter, greener leaves, which are delicious and more productive than the forced ones. For rhubarb I would force only when there are enough plants to allow for reduced growth the following year. If you want an earlier harvest when winter is cold, dig up a whole root in late autumn to grow under cover in darkness and warmth, as rhubarb growers do in commercial forcing sheds.

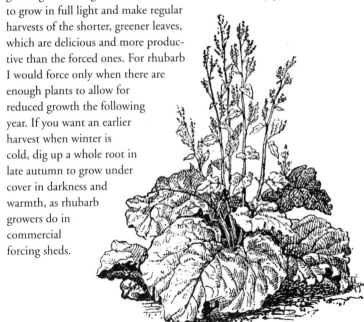

CHAPTER 7

MANURING AND FERTILIZING

Here we see how myths embody uncertain language: what is meant by manure and fertilizer, for example? There are also confusions about why we fertilize our gardens. As one clarifies the hidden assumptions and the meaning of terms, feeding plants becomes easier.

'Plants in healthy soil benefit from supplementary fertilizing and feeding.' *Untrue*

This belief has firm roots, but they are not in soil! For example, when showing slides of abundant growth in my gardens, stating clearly that I have added nothing to the soil except the compost to feed it, I am still asked if I have used fertilizers and which ones. Since the invention of synthetic fertilizers, the concept of feeding plants has overtaken that of nourishing the soil. An emphasis on plant nutrition means that soil is viewed mainly as a 'holding account' for nutrients, which come out of packets and bottles.

If you had little access to compost and manure, supplementary feeding would be a help in the short term, but I would also recommend buying a sack of compost for all its other attributes, such as conserving moisture and improving soil structure. It is only worth-while giving extra feeds for plants grown in containers and grow-bags, because of their restricted root runs, whereas I have never fed tomatoes rooted in open soil in polytunnels, and yields have always been good, with plants finding enough nutrients from the surface mulch of compost that I spread before planting. Furthermore, this soil carries enough goodness for a following crop of bountiful winter salads grown from autumn right through to spring.

❦

'Different plants need different approaches to manuring.' *Partly true*

This and many related myths have arisen out of confusing two vastly different approaches to encouraging growth: the use of synthetic fertilizers and the application of composts and animal manures.

Fertilizing soil in different ways for different plants is an approach that has been widely adopted, thanks to the ease and speed with which artificial, water-soluble fertilizer can be spread, with applications tailored to the perceived needs of each plant, according to the season and expected weather.

Organic gardening takes a different approach: you feed the *soil*, not the plant. This requires more effort (in handling compost and manure), but makes gardening much, much simpler and more enjoyable, with more freedom to change cropping ideas if the weather, seed quality or soil conditions necessitate a new plan. This is because *all* the soil benefits from feeding with organic matter every year, keeping its organisms active and healthy. They are then in the best condition to enable transfers of nutrients to whatever plants are growing, as needed. This often takes place via mycorrhizal fungi, which act as root extensions, foraging for nutrients and water in return for carbohydrates created by the plants' leaves.

'Soil nutrients are all water-soluble, washed down by rain and lost to plant roots.' *Untrue*

The widespread use of synthetic fertilizer, whose nutrients are mostly water soluble, gives credence to this belief; much pollution of groundwater has indeed resulted from the leaching of artificial fertilizers. But it is a statement that has been applied inappropriately to most soil and plant food, with the effect of undervaluing composts and composted manure, and discouraging their spreading at certain times of year.

Nutrients in compost and composted manure are much less water soluble than those in synthetic fertilizer. I demonstrate this every year by spreading composts in autumn and winter, leaving them on top of soil with no cover and with rain washing through. For all of the following year, growth is abundant, with second plantings also growing successfully without the addition of extra compost or fertilizer.

This myth is likely to be based on other assumptions too, for example that soil is cultivated every year. It may be that leaving soil undug and undisturbed helps soil life to keep nutrients temporarily locked up until they are needed by plants.

❧

'Giving precise nutrient feeds is key.' *Untrue*

J. Arthur Bower, who grew flowers commercially in the East of England from 1934 to the 1960s, had great success with using compost and nothing else from 1940. His produce commanded a 40-per-cent premium at markets because it was recognized for its better quality and for keeping longer. He wrote:

> The basic needs of plants are: (i) moisture, (ii) warmth, (iii) light. The question of nutrients is secondary to these; but it has been made the dominant one, and the most intricate of all. Why? Though I have been in horticulture now for 40 years, I don't think I should ever again want to try to match

my skill and experience against all the requirements of modern fertilizing. Such a way of going about things is too complicated and too risky. It calls for too many things to be done in a state of ignorance about the weather ahead and the level of available nutrients in the soil.

How much simpler it is to make compost by aerobic fermentation, and apply it to the land, leaving the rest of the job to the soil and its inhabitants. For 17 years, I have used no inorganic fertilizers of any kind on my holding.
(**Soil Association journal** *Mother Earth*, **1957**)

❦

'Liquid feeds made from leaves are smelly and pungent.' *Partly true*

Home-made liquid feeds, for example from leaves of comfrey and stinging nettles, have a stinky reputation, for good reason. I stopped using them because the ones I made, from soaking the leaves in water to extract their goodness, just gave off the worst kind of offensive odour. They even polluted the containers I soaked the leaves in, making them unpalatable for other uses.

Then I did a test, decomposing leaves without adding any water, by packing them in a large flower pot above a bucket, so that any juices could seep out of the hole in the bottom of the pot and accumulate in the bucket below. After a few weeks, I was delighted to find a decent amount of black liquid, *with no bad smell*, and the leaves had all collapsed into a dry mass in the pot above. This excellent plant feed needs diluting about 20:1 with water and is useful for any plants in containers.

'Overuse of manures makes soil acidic.' *Untrue*

Before the invention of chemical fertilizers, the only way of feeding plants was with animal manures, seaweed and rock dusts. Farmers often talked of 'manures' in a generic way, meaning 'plant food', and they have often transferred the use of the same word to manufactured fertilizer.

However, it avoids confusion to keep the word 'manure' for animal excretions mixed with bedding, 'compost' for decomposed organic matter of any kind (including animal manure), and 'fertilizer' for synthetic chemicals. Soil can indeed be made more acidic by careless or excessive use of man-made fertilizers, but not from spreading compost or manure.

Use of the word 'manure' for diametrically different products has caused many gardeners to believe that they must be unduly restrictive in using organic manures, even though these improve soil in so many ways, all without causing extra acidity. To illustrate: I asked a laboratory to compare the pH of two nearby soils. One was my beds, which had received 4cm (1½") of both my own compost and composted cow and horse manure every year for 11 years; the other was soil 45m (50 yards) away, which had received no compost or manure in that time. Both were pH 7.4.

❧

'You need to monitor and then adjust the feeding of plants as they grow.' *Untrue*

Soil has managed the seasonal flow of necessary nutrients in ages past, and plants have adapted to the supply system that has evolved around their roots. Trying to improve on this is possible, but requires the use of expensive, weather-dependent and water-soluble nutrient feeds, which sometimes leach into groundwater, and in healthy soil it is not necessary.

My own experience of using only compost is that nutrients become available when the correct temperature is reached, which is different for all plants: for example, spinach grows with dark green leaves in the low temperatures of early spring, but sweetcorn is yellow at that time because the nitrogen in the soil is unavailable to it, until warmer soil triggers sweetcorn's roots to interact with soil organisms and access the nutrients. When soil and weather conditions are wrong, applying soluble fertilizers is no help to plants and is a polluting waste; it is simpler and healthier (and cheaper in the long run) to apply composts, whose nutrients are available when needed, with little waste.

❧

'Green manures of leguminous plants always increase the nitrogen available to the next sowing and planting.' *Partly true*

Legumes are a good way of increasing available nitrogen in fields, where plants such as clover are growing for two or three years in swards of pasture, feeding animals and enriching the soil too. However, this statement concentrates on just one nutrient, and makes it sound easy to increase, but in gardening you must be clear about how long the legumes need to grow for, and whether you will remove them, leave them as a mulch or dig them in, and the consequences of each method.

For legumes to fix worthwhile amounts of nitrogen in a vegetable garden, where green manures are usually grown for less time than in fields, much care is needed. Plants will ideally be allowed to reach flowering stage, and their tops are then best removed to a compost heap, leaving just roots and nodules in the soil. This avoids having to cultivate to turn in the green matter, which would slow the subsequent growth of new plantings until the green manure's stems and leaves had been digested by soil, and avoids harming soil life such as mycorrhizal fungi (see page 78, 'You need to dig in order to expose soil pests for birds to eat them').

❧

'Sowing green manures is an easy way to conserve and build soil fertility in gardens.' *Untrue*

There are various factors to bear in mind when considering how easy this really is:

❧ Green manures' mass of leaf growth, as well as creating organic matter and hosting beneficial fauna, creates habitat for slugs.

❧ Weeds can gain a foothold among green manure plants, often going to seed, or, if perennial, establishing more roots, making it more difficult to grow the next vegetables.

❧ The decomposition of green manures in soil takes weeks rather than days, therefore if sowings or plantings are made too soon after mulching or incorporating them, their decaying leaves can draw nutrients away from plants that are trying to grow.

Albert Howard* called green manures a "many-sided biological problem likely to come into conflict with one rule in Nature after another". Howard emphasized that best results come from fast-growing, leafy green manures, for rapid decomposition, and that this is more likely in sandy soil than in clay, where a lack of air can result in slow or putrid decay. I find that where harvests are taken by early autumn, and as long as I don't want to plant another vege-table, sowings of mustard work well because they grow fast and the mustard plants are then killed by winter frosts, meaning that the organic matter decomposes on top and is taken in by worms.

*Sir Albert Howard (1873-1947) was an agricultural scientist and botanist who ran a research station in Indore, India, where his views developed on the value of traditional farming practices over the modern scientific approach. He was one of the Soil Association's founders in 1946, and his research was a corner-stone of early organic farmers' practices in Britain.

FEEDING SPECIFIC VEGETABLES

'You should not manure or compost soil where carrots and parsnips are to be sown.' *Untrue*

Confusion abounds here because of the unstated assumption that organic matter will be dug into soil, as most gardeners do, and this can result in forking as roots divert towards the pockets of uneven fertility. However, when compost and manures are left on the surface, and seeds such as carrot and parsnip are sown into this organic matter, there is no particular forking and growth is strong, with high yields of roots. I use this approach every year, growing mostly straight roots of good quality.

'Root vegetables need no feeding.' *Partly true*

This is too simply worded and makes sense only for nitrogen fertilizer, which encourages more leaf than root. But all parts of a plant need to function together, and you can't have large roots without large leaves. This understanding contributes to a simpler approach, whereby rather than 'targeted feeding' you can feed all the soil with organic matter each year (see page 61, and also page 43, 'Overfed onions are all leaf and no root').

'Legume vegetables do not need compost because they provide their own nitrogen.' *Partly true*

This advice often crops up in explanations of managing crop rotation, with most compost and manure recommended for the potato quarter, and some for brassicas. It is not wrong advice, but places too much emphasis on the value of nitrogen, which is only one of the many nutrients needed. This myth is correctly contradicted by the next – which is, however, misleading for a different reason.

❧

'Climbing beans need to be grown in a trench filled with organic matter.' *Untrue*

This is just one of many ways to grow a fast-growing vegetable that needs plenty of nutrients and moisture. But climbing beans also grow well in undug, surface-composted soil, where the organic matter on top holds moisture and feeds the soil below, as well as encouraging worms, whose channels of movement are then available to roots for their foraging through soil to considerable depth.

CHAPTER 8

MAKING AND USING COMPOST

Much lore has accumulated around the subject of making compost: some of it is mythical and best composted itself! You can compost many garden ingredients that are often recommended to be left out of the heap, and you can make good compost without heat.

'You cannot safely compost rhubarb leaves or citrus peel.' *Untrue*

This myth about rhubarb leaves probably originated because of the high levels of oxalic acid they contain, which makes them poisonous to eat. Yet this is no problem for a compost heap, where digestion is so powerful: the acid is broken down and the leaves turn into valuable humus.

Citrus peel also has a bad name, perhaps because brandling (compost) worms do not appreciate it in wormeries, but I have always added the household's citrus peel to compost heaps and it turns into compost. The only difficulty might be if the oranges and lemons have been waxed to give them shelf life and a glossy look, but they do break down eventually; unwaxed organic citrus fruit disappears faster.

'You cannot safely compost roots of bindweed and other perennial weeds.' *Untrue*

Actually you can, as long as the roots have no chance to re-grow until they have exhausted their resources from trying, so they just need to be starved of light. This is easy when they are buried by regular filling of a heap – just keep perennial weed roots away from heap edges if they allow some light in, and keep the lid on a sealed bin. Summer warmth and regular filling also help a heap to achieve temperatures where decay happens more quickly.

I add roots of docks, nettles, dandelion, couch grass and bindweed to my heaps and they all turn to compost, with just the occasional one re-growing if it is close to any gaps in the sides, say between the planks of a pallet. Should that happen, it is simple to pull out the growing roots when compost is either turned or spread, and this approach is altogether easier and quicker than other remedies, such as soaking roots in water until they are rotten.

❧

'You cannot safely compost potato and tomato plants infected with blight.' *Untrue*

What is mostly referred to as 'blight' is 'late blight', *Phytopthora infestans*, and it causes so much damage to potato and tomato plants that its powers have become almost mythical themselves. However, there are strict limits to the conditions in which late blight can develop: moisture on leaves, air humidity above 90 per cent and night temperatures above 10°C (50°F) for two days at least (known as a 'Smith period' – see page 87). Key to avoiding the disease on tomatoes under cover is by watering the soil and compost only from midsummer, to keep their leaves dry (see page 43, in 'You can't grow cucumbers and tomatoes together'). But however we manage our gardens, in sufficiently wet and warm conditions late blight will infect outdoor potato and tomato plants at some point in the summer, from spores that multiply in their millions and float in on the wind.

I have always composted all my blighted leaves, fruits and tubers of tomato and potato. It helps that heaps fill fast in late summer and autumn, when the blighted debris is decomposing. In spring the resulting compost can be spread wherever needed: I sometimes use it in polytunnels where tomatoes are then planted, and they grow healthily without blight; I have also grown healthy potatoes near to where I had grown blighted ones the year before (see also page 87).

❧

'You cannot make good compost if the heap is never hot.' *Untrue*

Hot compost happens where there is enough aerated 'green' and 'brown' matter to feed rapidly multiplying bacteria, whose work of decomposition generates heat, often up to 60°C (140°F), which is sufficient to kill weed seeds and disease pathogens (see also page 89). However, this level of heat can also kill some useful fungi, such that compost from heaps which have been turned regularly by machines to mix ingredients and introduce more air, causing temperatures to rise even higher than 60°C, is often black and relatively lifeless compared with mouldering domestic compost.

You can make excellent compost in heaps that rarely warm up to hand-hot – the composting process just takes longer and is orches-trated by fungi instead of bacteria. These fungi are hugely beneficial when they multiply in soil, helping plants to access nutrients and also water.

Compost made under cooler temperatures may be lumpy and sticky until a year old, but when it is spread and left on the soil surface in autumn, air and weather help to finish breaking it down, and it becomes a soft planting medium by spring.

❧

'You need to add worms to compost heaps.'
Untrue

Maturing compost is quickly colonized by legions of red brandling worms, even when heaps are built on hard-standing. Presumably the worm eggs are in the soil that we add to our compost heaps, on plant and weed roots. Every heap I have ever made has filled with worms as it matures, so I would never waste time adding any.

❧

'Slatted sides are best, to let air in.' *Untrue*

Although air is a vital ingredient, little *new* air can enter through holes in a heap's sides, because the ingredients block its passage: hence the value of turning a heap. I have noticed no difference between solid and slatted sides, finding that sides of 12mm (½") plywood work well, being quick to assemble, light to move, and retaining warmth and moisture at the heap's edges.

❧

'Heaps must be sited in shade / full sunlight.'
Untrue

It is sometimes claimed that tree shade helps the composting pro-cess, and perhaps it does, but it is a small factor. At other times, one reads that 'heaps must be in full sun to capture its warmth'! Heaps can be sited anywhere really: I have made lovely compost under overhanging pine trees, and I have made lovely compost in full sunlight!

'Heaps need to be inoculated with an activator.' *Partly true*

Yes, it is possible to speed up and improve the composting process with proprietary or home-made herbal additions to heaps. However, you can also make excellent compost with just weeds and plant debris. Adding any manure of hamsters, rabbits and chickens is a cheap and effective way to make even better compost.

MYTHS ABOUT SOWING AND GROWING IN COMPOST

'Plants can be damaged by an excess of nutrients in compost.' *Untrue*

I am frequently asked whether plants can be 'burned', meaning overwhelmed, by an excess of nutrients in compost, but this cannot happen because compost is the result of a process that stabilizes nutrient availability.

Therefore composts, whether made from decomposed plant or animal manure, provided that they have had no synthetic nutrients added, cannot damage plants with an excess of food. The process of composting involves the creation of soft humus, which holds nutrients in a stable, water-insoluble form, ready for use by plants when fungal interactions send the right messages. Fortunately for us gardeners, such biological mechanisms look after plant feeding and growth without us needing to worry or be involved, especially in soils, where compost is providing food for the hordes of bacteria and fungi. (See also page 61, 'Different plants need different approaches to manuring' and page 82, 'You should not sow seeds into manure'.)

'Seedling roots can suffer burns when sown or planted into composts spread on soil.' *Untrue*

Although similar to the previous myth, and also to the one about sowing into manures (page 82), this one is subtly different. The main thing to know is that you can sow into any compost that is physically crumbly enough, even if only recently spread, although sowing into weathered, older compost is easier. In 30 years of sowing seeds into compost on the soil surface, of many kinds and of different maturities and in varying depths, I have never experienced poor growth from nutrient excesses or imbalances; only occasionally from sowing into a thicker mulch of more woody, green-waste compost, when plants' leaves went temporarily yellow from nutrient shortage.

Every year I am intrigued to compare the growth of seeds between two of my experimental beds, one of which is dug in autumn, with compost incorporated and therefore seeds sown into the soil, and the other left undug with the compost on top. Seeds all germinate and grow well on both beds, until differences appear in a few weeks – with about half the vegetables, especially spinach, lettuce, onions and parsnips, showing a preference for starting off in compost, while cabbages, potatoes and carrots sometimes look stronger in the dug soil.

❧

'Compost tea is a nutrient feed.' *Untrue*

There is a mistaken idea that 'compost tea' means the dark liquids that seep out of compost and manure heaps, which look rich but may contain more carbon than nutrients, and may be unhealthily anaerobic. True compost tea is a recently invented brew of microorganisms rather than nutrients. It is made by adding a small amount of high-quality compost to a large quantity of water and some sugars, such as molasses, to feed billions of microorganisms, multiplied by mechanical stirring and oxygenation for up to 24 hours. It is not a nutrient feed but a brew containing vast amounts of fungi and bacteria, which can be formulated according to the required results, from an abundance of vegetables to impressive golf greens.

Compost teas' richness of life can unlock the goodness in moribund soils, and results from using it on nutrient-rich but low-yielding soils are remarkable, as discovered, for example, by Gareth Cameron of the National Vegetable Society when his pot leeks, which had stopped responding to applications of fertilizer, grew again after he sprayed compost tea on his soil.[9]

❧

'Organic potting composts have a lower nutrient content.' *Partly true*

While this may be true, it is not a problem, because the nutrients in organic composts are rationed by being less water-soluble. This has two results: firstly, leaf growth is smaller but stronger and less susceptible to aphids; secondly, less of the nutrient content is leached out and lost if the compost is overwatered.

The composts to avoid are those with too many woody bits. I noticed this in a comparison of lettuces growing in four different composts, one of which had plenty of shredded wood visible. Its lettuce plant barely grew, while those in multipurpose compost, cow manure and garden compost all thrived. (All the plants were strong and healthy when first planted into the composts.) Leaves of the woody-compost lettuce stayed pink or purple rather than green: a sure sign of 'nitrogen robbery' by the wood, until after three months there was a hint of green, as the wood was finishing its decomposition and using up less nitrogen, allowing some for the lettuce.

Fortunately, using woody compost as a *surface* mulch in the garden has little of this effect because there is minimal wood in contact with the soil.

'Proprietary seed composts are best for getting seeds started.' *Untrue*

If only this *were* true . . . but I have made surprising discoveries about what seeds do like to emerge in. Proprietary composts for propagation are based either on loam (soil), peat or composted plant matter such as bark, leaves and general green waste, which often includes some woody bits. A variable amount of nutrients is added, according to the proposed use of the compost. Seed or sowing compost has the least added nutrients, to prevent 'burning' of seedlings, which shows as poor emergence and some little seedlings turning a dark colour before dying off.

I have had more problems with germination in proprietary seed composts than in ordinary multipurpose mixes. The only vegetables I have known to 'burn' – in some dense, multipurpose compost, where lack of air was more harmful than nutrient excess – are beetroot, spinach and lettuce. I find that beetroot emerges best in a mix of half cow manure, half home-made compost, both about 18 months old and including bits of brown straw, which allow water to percolate through. This rich compost grows big, strong plants, demonstrating that successful growth is as much about good drainage for germinating seedlings as about the amounts of nutrients present.

CHAPTER 9

SOIL STRUCTURE AND CARE

In books and articles about gardening, it is often assumed that soil is improved by regular loosening. "Digging the soil is essential for good plant growth," we are told on the BBC website as I write this book. It's worth taking a closer look at the reasons usually given.

'Tillage is good for soil.' *Untrue*

Loosening soil with tools and machines has some inconvenient results:

- An increase in weed seeds germinating.
- An increase in perennial weed numbers, from the regrowth of chopped roots.
- A loss of moisture as soil is exposed to drying winds.
- A loss of organic matter, from carbon going into the atmosphere as carbon dioxide.
- Damage to and death of soil inhabitants such as worms, beetles, bacteria and in particular mycorrhizal fungi (see next myth).
- A loss of existing soil structure, such that compaction becomes more likely, which necessitates further tillage.

Sometimes digging is useful to bury thick growth of grass and weeds, as a first stage in having clean soil for sowing. From then on, however, it works to copy the natural process whereby untilled soil stays healthy and aerated, preferably with new 'food' on top. I have done this on soils ranging from stony brash to dense, white clay, with successful growth in all cases. For vegetables especially, you need to add some organic matter to grow good plants, but less is needed in the long term than if soil is tilled, because there is reduced oxidation of carbon from untilled soil, and carbon is the building block of organic matter.

❦

'You need to dig in order to expose soil pests for birds to eat them.' *Untrue*

This bizarre statement seems to assume that soil contains only pests and problems, such as slug eggs, which can be exposed in tillage, but this benefit is far outweighed by the damage to beneficial organisms:

- ❦ Earthworms are exposed to predatory birds, if they have not already been chopped in half by a spade. Earthworms play a major role in recycling organic matter and plant food, improving soil structure through their nutrient-rich and well-structured excretions – in short, doing many of the jobs that are supposed to be performed by digging.
- ❦ Mycorrhizal fungae are killed by exposure to air, thus reducing the potential growth of all plants in the dug soil, until the mycorrhizae have recolonized (after about six months, from the results of my experiments).
- ❦ Many soil organisms are disrupted, for example black ground beetles, which feed on insects, slugs and weed seeds: just one member of a complex community of soil life that we'd do well to leave alone.
- ❦ Rather than turning soil, I would turn this myth on its head . . .

'In order to maintain healthy soil life, and nutrients in a stable structure, you need to *not* dig.'
True!

Soil fauna are less obvious and less discussed than the larger animals and insects around us, but are just as important and repay a gardener's care with healthier growth of plants. A large ingredient of soil fertility is healthy and active soil life – the myriad visible and microscopic soil organisms that are continually moving and eating in the soil, helping to recycle nutrients and maintain and improve soil structure, all playing a part in maintaining the balance of pests and predators.

I wish we *could* see the myriad small organisms in soil, because they make such an important contribution to healthy growth.

Penelope Hobhouse, gardener, designer and author of many books on ornamental gardens, told me that she has found that her plants grow fine in uncultivated soil. She creates new ornamental gardens in undisturbed, mulched soil, using weedkiller as a first step, with much less time and energy needed for subsequent weeding and watering.

❧

'You need to provide loose soil for parsnip and carrot roots to go down.' *Untrue*

With some compost on top to maintain structure below, carrots and parsnips go straight down into undisturbed soil, even clay. The problem is less about getting them to grow; more about how to extract their long roots, which does require some soil loosening.

After the harvest of long roots, unless soil is thoroughly wet, I tread or walk on the bed to firm it down again. This keeps soil firm and homogeneous, without excess dry air, which is harmful to some organisms.

'Gardeners need to aerate soil for plants to make healthy roots.' *Untrue*

Seeds need air in soil to germinate, and roots need air too, as well as room to grow, but all this can happen without any soil loosening by the gardener. Roots travel happily in soil that may *look* dense but is in fact full of air channels and spaces between large and small aggregations of soil excreted by different organisms. When harvesting long parsnips and examining clay on the lower part of their roots, I find that it reveals a crumbly structure when subjected to pressure, owing to the excretions generated by soil organisms.

❧

'Digging reduces compaction.' *True but misleading*

This statement hides a linguistic confusion between the words 'firm' and 'compact', with healthily firm soil often described as compacted. Plants like firm soil, and root into a wide range of undisturbed soil types and structures, but how do you know if the soil in your plot is compacted rather than naturally firm? If weed growth is abundant and water drains after rain, you can be confident that there is no problem; otherwise, dig a small hole to the depth of a spade to check for any putrid smells and for orange and grey zones of airlessness. If these are prevalent, you could dig once, and, for a longer-term solution, spread extra organic matter on top after digging.

❧

'Seeds and plants need really fine soil for sowing and planting.' *Mostly untrue*

In practice it works well to have a range of particle size in the soil, because fine soil can slump together in rain and then form a capping layer of hard soil on top when dry. Well-decomposed organic matter, such as one-year-old compost and manure, is excellent for sowing into (see page 74), as indeed are the composts you can buy, when spread as a surface mulch. All seeds like the soft moistness of compost, and grow well with some lumps in the seedbed; even small seeds such as carrots.

'You should never walk on your beds.' *Untrue*

This advice arises from the management of tilled plots, where the soil structure is regularly broken up and the soil is therefore unable to support weight without collapsing and losing much of the air introduced by cultivation. Soil that is undisturbed and fed with a thin layer of organic matter on top has a firm rather than compact structure, full of worm channels and so forth, which can support weight. At the same time, plant roots can travel through it – much as in lawns that we walk on.

'In wet weather, always use a plank when walking on soil.' *Untrue*

As with the previous myth, this applies only to dug soil, which is soft and liable to damage from any weight in wet weather. I can push wheelbarrows over my undug clay even when wet, and also find that the mud sticks less to the boots, so I have access to the growing area in all weathers. This has been a vital part of my market-gardening business in wet seasons: I have not lost time due to rain and mud, and can harvest, plant, remove weeds and spread compost whatever the weather.

'Compost and manure is best incorporated into the root zone.' *Untrue*

This statement contradicts natural processes in two ways. Firstly, soil organisms have evolved to seek and pull down organic matter from above. Secondly, many plant roots feed at the surface. Organic matter left on the surface breaks down gradually into food for soil and plants, more easily than when dug in, thanks to free availability of the air required for final decomposition. It is incorporated in the end, all for free and with no harm to any soil life.

❧

'You should not sow seeds into manure,' or 'Manure burns seedlings.' *Partly true*

Confusion arises here because of misunderstandings about manure. Only fresh manure might cause damage to plants, because damage to small seedlings can happen if there is excessive nutrient availability, but I have never actually experienced it in the thousands of sowings I have made into manure. The only difficulties have been to do with creating a tilth, which is easier when manure has spent a couple of months on the soil surface to soften up, after which it makes an excellent sowing medium for all seeds, including carrots and parsnips (see page 67).

Unfounded worries abound, such as this post on my forum: "The nursery lady informed me that mushroom compost must be incorporated, otherwise it will burn the plants' roots." Another gardener asked me whether you really can plant into year-old manure, because "Surely there is too much nitrogen, which burns the roots, and too much carbon, which pulls nutrients way from roots?". In fact those two statements cancel each other out: there is a plant-friendly balance of nitrogen and carbon in year-old manure, and nutrients in organic materials are not free to dissolve in water, so causing no harm to plant roots.

❧

'Dug soil dries and warms up more quickly than undug soil.' *Untrue*

Undug soil does indeed dry more slowly than dug soil, which means that it is in fact warmer at night, because moisture holds heat; also, undisturbed soil can conduct warmth from *below*. In his book *The Weed Problem*, F. C. King* quoted the results of a trial by the Scottish Fruit Growers' Research Association in 1948: during frosty weather, the temperature of undisturbed wet loam was -3.2°C (26.3°F), compared with -3.9°C (24.9°F) on an adjacent plot that had been tilled to a depth of 7.5cm (3").[10]

❧

'Digging increases fertility.' *Untrue*

This vague promise was also addressed by F. C. King, whose curiosity led him to run trials using organic matter in two ways: incorporated while digging, or spread on top of undisturbed soil.[11] He concluded that "because repeated cultivations tend to *increase*

---

* F. C. King was head gardener on the 10 acres of Levens Hall in Cumbria in the 1930s and 1940s, with an increasing use of no-dig and surface-composting methods, resulting in Levens Hall becoming a place of pilgrimage for gardeners interested in how to make and use compost. King's *Gardening with Compost* was published in 1944 (republished in 2002).

the rate of consumption of organic fragments, the less we dig, the longer our supply of humus will last", and "soils which have not been dug for many years are better aerated than similar soils which have been regularly inverted by the spade".[12] Nowadays he could add that less carbon escapes from untilled soil.

❦

'Adding sand to clay helps drainage and aeration.' *Partly true*

Although this sounds correct, and you can introduce air if you somehow manage to mix sand into clay, there is no guarantee of better soil quality in the long run. With the amounts normally recommended, about 25kg for 5m (55lb for 16') of bed, sand can turn clay into a good ingredient for making bricks. An easier way to improve aeration and drainage is by adding organic matter, preferably on top, to feed worms who then bring stable air channels into the soil; also, organic matter adds fertility, whereas sand or gravel contribute only volume.

CHAPTER 10

PESTS, DISEASES
AND WEEDS

The key to coping with pests, diseases and weeds is a sound understanding of how, where and why they flourish; then of how to remove and prevent them. Once you can see the confusions in the myths that abound on this subject, your garden can be cleaner and healthier, for less effort and expense.

PESTS AND DISEASES

'Insecticides made from natural materials are not toxic.' *Untrue*

An insecticide kills living organisms and, whatever its origin, it is poisonous. So-called organic pesticides can create a false sense of safety, one example being derris powder, which is made from roots of the derris plant, but is toxic to fish and many other organisms as well as to the caterpillars and aphids it is used to kill.

Using organic pesticides can put the farmer and gardener in the same dangerous place of wanting to *fight problems* rather than seeking to *manage and minimize* them. Gardeners should have little or no need for pesticides, and should accept instead that there are always a few pests. To reduce pests, you can learn the optimum time for sowing different seeds, and take advantage of the fact that pests impact less on plants when the soil is fertile. Plant diversity also helps: it not only leads to an increase in predators of pests, but plants also like it (a 'companion effect' – but see below). You can also use protective barriers against pests in some cases.

❦

'Grow companion plants to prevent pest damage.'
Partly true

I love companion planting and do it a lot, but I use the word 'prevent' in this myth to make the point that companion planting is not on a par with using a pesticide, although it is often presented as an equivalent alternative. It is correct, much of the time, to say that companion planting *reduces* pest damage, but other factors always play a part, and in years when conditions are favourable for particular pests, they are difficult to control by any means.

I have had whitefly on tomatoes with French marigolds (*Tagetes patula*) interplanted, carrot root fly where onions were sown with carrots, and couch grass continuing to grow between my plants of tall Mexican marigolds (*Tagetes minuta*). Sometimes the companion plants have helped, and they certainly give predators more chance to find host plants and favourable conditions, so that a balance is found. 'Balance' is the key word to remember: every garden needs a few pests, otherwise it cannot provide a home for any predators and the ecosystem is less stable. If a toad eats all your slugs, he or she may have to move away.

❦

'Greenhouses need sterilizing at the end of each growing season.' *Untrue*

The important point here is that most of the living organisms that surround us in our gardens are beneficial, so a big risk of any sterilizing is that more useful insects and other organisms perish than 'bad' ones. Ladybirds, spiders, centipedes and beetles are all friends to the gardener and we should hope they survive winter, in order to breed and continue their helpful lives through the following years.

A good example of an absence of predator control is the increase in numbers of aphids every spring ahead of the arrival of new predator offspring, until a balance is found – just as long as a few predators have indeed survived the winter. I recommend that you leave greenhouses and polytunnels well alone except for two things: firstly, clean the glass or plastic, so that as much light as possible can enter, using just water with a little vinegar; secondly, clear any overgrowing plants and old wood, to reduce the habitat for slugs and woodlice respectively.

❦

'Spores of potato blight can survive in the soil.'
Untrue

The usual recommendation is to burn blighted leaves, fruits and tubers, and this arises from a worry that blight can survive the winter in compost and soil. Fortunately, this is not the case in the UK (see page 70), although the disease evolves continually. To overwinter, blight requires living plant tissue, which means that infected potato tubers are its only resting place, because all blighted leaves and stems die in winter frosts. I have had 'early blight' (*Alternaria solani*) on first early potatoes, from infected tubers; thankfully, this is less vigorous than 'late blight' (*Phytopthora infestans*).

Blight spores reproduce only in humid and warm conditions, with damaging increases in any 'Smith period' – when, for two consecutive days and nights, the air temperature is always above 10°C (50°F), and the relative humidity is 90 per cent for at least a quarter of that time. Such conditions can occur from the middle of June in the UK, and more often in a wet July, when the destructive 'late blight' can appear suddenly. In suitable conditions, it multiplies so fast and spreads so widely on the wind that keeping potato and tomato leaves dry is the only solution, so the spores have no landing place.

'Plant diseases are contagious.' *Mostly untrue*

It is encouraging to know that most plant diseases are specific to certain plants and usually also to other members of their family, but not to plants in general. For example, all alliums are susceptible to *Puccinia allii* rust on their leaves, and this rust can spread between alliums to some extent, but does not infect other plants. Rust spots on the leaves of plants in other families may look the same but they are different types of rust, for example infecting only broad bean or maize leaves respectively.

A second point is that diseases generally take hold when conditions are favourable to them and when plants are less able to resist them for some reason. So, for example, mildew on spinach and lamb's lettuce (corn salad) in dry weather is a result of dry soil stressing plants, whose weaker leaves then succumb to infection by mildew spores, which are commonly lurking but can only develop in favourable conditions on weaker leaves. Like slugs, mildew spores are part of nature's cycle of growth and decay, and when we keep plants healthy and growing, they are less susceptible to the many possible diseases.

The most aggravating disease, late blight on potatoes and tomatoes, cannot develop on dry leaves. Other leaf diseases can be controlled with some extra watering (in the case of dry weather mildews), removing crowded leaves (in the case of damp weather mildews) and generally by keeping plants tidy, because decaying leaves attract diseases. For example, you can remove all old brassica leaves to the compost heap. I find that leaving soil undug also helps, because cultivating the soil can spread the spores of some fungal diseases, such as white rot, over larger areas.

WEEDS

'Weed seeds can be killed in domestic compost heaps.' *Mostly untrue*

I do not want to discourage gardeners from composting everything
they can, but weed seeds are an issue! I have rarely found that garden-
scale compost heaps, say 1.5m² (16ft sq), can generate and sustain
enough heat to kill more than half of the weed seeds I have
included as ingredients. There is just too much cooling effect near
a heap's edges, and even when these are then turned to the middle,
there is too little fresh green matter to generate enough new heat.

Turning a heap works well for making lovely compost, but weed
seeds tend to survive it. If you don't want weeds, however, there is
a way: to discourage annual weeds from germinating, use mulches,
especially of clean composts, which are available to buy; for example mushroom compost and green-waste compost. This gives you
time to hoe or pull out the reduced number of weeds when small,
long before they can flower and set seed. Your own compost will
then contain few weed seeds and you can enjoy using it more.

❦

'Regular hoeing keeps soil aerated, mulched and less weedy.' *Partly true*

My mother used to say this and I believed her at the time, but now
I think she hadn't tried the other ways of aerating soil. Undoubtedly
there is some value in hoeing: where masses of weed seedlings do
germinate, it is the quickest and simplest way to be rid of them,
when they are tiny and almost before you can see them. But hoeing
is not for aeration or mulching, which is best achieved with the
application of compost, and I have found growth to be as good, if
not better, without regular hoeing around plants.

The main need for weekly or fortnightly hoeing occurs after soil is
dug over. F. C. King (see page 83) described this when he wrote:
"For each hour that we use the spade, we must use the hoe for four

hours. Once we cease to dig, the need for a hoe becomes less insistent."[13] He knew this because he dared to leave an area undug, and then noticed its lesser weed growth compared with nearby dug soil.

❧

'Bare soil inevitably has many annual weeds germinating.' *Untrue*

Weeds do not appear out of thin air, however much it may seem so. The statement above is a disempowering one, because with good garden practice, weeds become markedly less common: reduce soil disturbance and you find that annual weeds germinate less readily. The main time when weeds grow is during the first year of starting a garden on new ground, where there are often many perennial weeds, and residual weed seeds from years past, which germinate in cleared soil unless a light-excluding mulch is used.

Mulching and hoeing in the first year is the first stage of reducing weeds and viable seeds at surface level, such that bare soil does not re-cover with weeds. When I left behind my old gardens at Lower Farm, I noticed how clean the untended soil remained for several months, such that one could have quickly had a clean seedbed at any time, after removing a few grass and thistle plants. Compared with cultivated soil, undisturbed soil is in a calmer state and has less need to re-cover itself (or to recover, for that matter).

❧

'Growth of moss indicates acid soil.' *Untrue*

I have often heard this said, but doubted it when noticing moss on some pathways of my alkaline (pH 7.4) soil, and I have noticed that moss grows anywhere it finds soil that is damp and mild for long enough. So it thrives in wet summers, and also where there is some shade, as in shady lawns, and where soil is firm, as in damp pathways. If you are troubled by moss, it can be hoed off in dry weather or raked out of lawns, and composted. It may be sheltering slugs, but in itself is not harmful.

TIPS FOR AVOIDING / MANAGING PESTS, DISEASES AND WEEDS

For all these garden problems, information and understanding are key. Knowing which pests are likely, such as slugs on salads in wet soil and caterpillars on summer brassicas, gives you a chance to prepare, by having soil in its best condition and crop covers ready to protect against particular insects. Some pests can be avoided by timing sowings so that plants will encounter fewer of the pests that normally damage them: for example, sow brassica salads (rocket, mustards, pak choi, mizuna) in late summer rather than spring.

❦

Many plant diseases follow rhythms of growth where leaves weaken towards the end of a cycle, as with mildew on lettuce and Cucurbitaceae leaves in autumn. Recognizing the inevitability of such diseases helps you understand that often there is no need to worry about damage to leaves. On the other hand, you need to recognise and know about certain toxic diseases, such as white rot on alliums, the control of which is more complex. I find that a three- or four-year gap before growing more alliums, growing brassicas before the next alliums, and not digging soil, all help.

❦

Weeds can be cleared completely and then kept under control by understanding which weeds you have and how they grow, so you can use the most effective method of either mulching, hoeing or pulling (or all three), and at the right time. Next, you need to recognize and understand the growth pattern of a few highly invasive weeds, such as marestail (*Conyza canadensis*), which are almost impossible to eradicate but can be kept at bay. Other invasives, such as couch grass (*Elymus repens*), can be eradicated, but you need to be systematic.

INDEX